A History of Scotland Book

MODERN TIMES

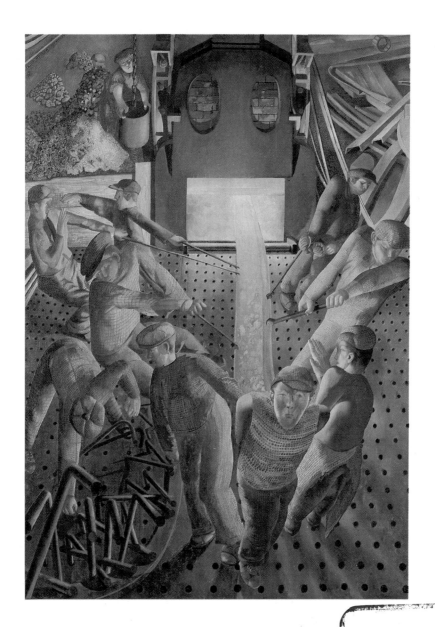

Alastair McIntosh Gray

Oxford University Press 1989

*Oxford University Press, Walton Street,
Oxford OX2 6DP*

Oxford New York Toronto
Delhi Bombay Calcutta Madras Karachi
Petaling Jaya Singapore Hong Kong Tokyo
Nairobi Dar es Salaam Cape Town
Melbourne Auckland

and associated companies in
Berlin Ibadan

Oxford is a trade mark of Oxford University Press

© Alastair McIntosh Gray 1989

British Library Cataloguing in Publication Data

Gray, Alastair McIntosh, 1953–
    A History of Scotland.
    Bk. 5
    1. Scotland. History – For schools
    I. Title
    941.1
    ISBN 0-19-917064-9 (Hardback)
    ISBN 0-19-917063-0 (Paperback)

Typeset by Pentacor Ltd., High Wycombe, Bucks

Printed in Hong Kong

Acknowledgements

The Publisher would like to thank the following for permission to reproduce photographs:

Aberdeen Art Gallery and Museums p. 142 top; Aberdeen Libraries p. 42; Aberdeen University Library p. 20; Aerofilms p. 85 top, 116 right, 129 left; Alban Pictures p. 29 right, 115, 120, 121, 134 top; Alcan Chemicals Ltd. p. 33; Walter Alexander and Co. Ltd. p. 90; Ian Allan Ltd. p. 24; Nic Allen/Moubray House Press p. 23 bottom; Ancient Art and Architecture Collection p. 104 left; T. and R. Annan and Sons p. 44 bottom; Ash Gupta Ltd. p. 31 inset; Sophie Baker/RSC p. 41; B. T. Batsford Ltd. p. 31 bottom; BBC Enterprises p. 139 top left, top right; BBC Scotland p. 139 centre left, centre right; BBC Hulton Picture Library p. 22, 37 top, 51, 73 right, 96 bottom; British Coal p. 103; The British Library p. 59, 76 bottom, 84 top, 100 bottom, 104 right, 111 top right, 135 centre; British Petroleum p. 112 top left; Camera Press p. 127 top left; Central Office of Information p. 80; Chicago Tribune p. 50; The Church of Scotland p. 127 top right; Clydebank District Libraries p. 6; J. and P. Coats Ltd. p. 5 top right, centre left; David Cochran p. 8 top right, 45 top, 56, 70, 71 bottom, 101 right, 113 right, 119 right, 126 left, 128; Colorsport p. 118 top; Constable and Co. Ltd. p. 140 centre right; Fidelity Dean p. 14 bottom, 100 top; Don-Mor Productions p. 133; Dundee District Libraries p. 14 top, 37 bottom; Dundee Museums and Art Galleries p. 4; Edinburgh City Libraries p. 25 bottom, 29 left, 31 top; Edinburgh Photo Library p. 30 top, 32 bottom, 86, 127 centre left, 131 right, 138, 140 bottom right; Mary Evans Picture Library p. 7, 13, 28, 72; Forbo-Nairn Ltd. p. 5 top left; Forestry Commission, Edinburgh p. 87, 136 left; Gillanders and Mack p. 45 bottom; Glasgow District Libraries p. 19 bottom, 46 bottom; The Glasgow Herald p. 11, 53, 55, 60, 62, 63, 64 bottom, 68, 75, 76 top, 95, 97 bottom right, 104 top, 111 bottom left, 122 top, 129 right, 140 top left; Glasgow Museums and Art Galleries/The Burrell Collection p. 44 bottom, 78; Glasgow Museums and Art Galleries/Art Gallery and Museum, Kelvingrove p. 43 bottom; Glasgow Museums and Art Galleries/ Museum of Transport p. 89; Glasgow Museums and Art Galleries/People's Palace p. 16 top left, 18, 48 top, 65 top left, 94 bottom, 97 bottom left, 98; Glasgow University Archives p. 8 bottom, 9 centre; Govan Shipbuilders p. 109 right; Alastair McIntosh Gray p. 127 centre right, 136 bottom, 137 top left, top right; Robert Harding Picture Library p. 135 top, 142 bottom; House of Fraser Collection/Glasgow University Archives p. 137 bottom; Imperial War Museum p. 54 bottom, 58, 61, 99; Inverness Museum and Art Gallery p. 91; Rhian Irith p. 90 centre; Michael Jenner p. 34; 'Alain Le Garsmeur/Impact p. 136 right; The Labour Party Library p. 102; Le Corbusier and Jeanneret, 'Voisin' plan of Paris 1925, The Museum of Modern Art, New York p. 123 centre; Lipton Export Ltd. p. 16 top right, bottom left; Norman MacKenzie p. 84 bottom; Oscar Marzaroli p. 124; Sam Maynard p. 82; Marie McKinney p. 103 bottom; Gunnie Moberg p. 96 top, centre; Moubray House Press p. 23 bottom; National Film Archive, London p. 140 top right; National Gallery of Scotland p. 43 top; National Portrait Gallery p. 40 left; National Railway Museum p. 88; Copyright © 1929 The New York Times Company. Reprinted by permission p. 65 bottom; New Zealand Ship and Marine Society/Dumbarton Public Library p. 10; The Orkney Library p. 54 top, 92; Eduardo Paolozzi/The Ruskin School of Drawing p. 141 bottom left; Popperfoto p. 9 right, 21, 48 bottom, 57, 66, 69, 94 top, 101 top, 105; P. R. Consultants Scotland p. 132; Radio Times p. 73 left; Rolls Royce plc p. 97 top; Royal Commission on Ancient Monuments, Scotland p. 27; Royal Geographical Society p. 9 left; Royal Incorporation of Architects in Scotland p. 67, 69 top right; Science Photo Library p. 101 centre; The Scotsman p. 100 bottom, 106, 107 left, right, 109 left, 111 top left, 112 top right, 113 left, 114 top, 116 left, 117, 118 bottom, 119 left, 122 bottom, 123 bottom; Scotrail p. 131 left; Scottish Film Archive/Films of Scotland Collection p. 81; Scottish Mountaineering Club p. 35 left; Scottish National Party p. 107 top right; Scottish National Portrait Gallery p. 79; Scottish Opera p. 141 top right; Scottish Tourist Board p. 35 right; Tom Scott p. 49, 140 bottom left; Line illustration copyright Ernest H. Shepard under the Berne Convention, copyright in colouring-in of illustrations © 1970, 1971 by Ernest Shepard and Methuen Children's Books Ltd. p. 26; Hank Snoek/Sir Basil Spence, Glover and Ferguson p. 125; Tom Steel/Scotland's Story Collection p. 36 right; Strathclyde Regional Archives p. 10 centre, 17, 36 left, 38, 74; Charles Swithinbank p. 9 top; Syndication International p. 108, 126 right; The Tate Gallery p. 141 bottom right; Telefocus p. 47; Eileen Tweedy/The Conservative Party p. 114 bottom left; Weidenfeld and Nicolson Ltd. p. 85 bottom; Marie West p. 15; The Wick Society p. 30 bottom; Adam Woolfitt/Susan Griggs p. 112 bottom; The World Conference p. 19 top right; Illustration by N. C. Wyeth from 'Kidnapped'. Copyright 1913 Charles Scribner's Sons, copyright renewed. Reproduced with the permission of Charles Scribner's Sons, a division of Macmillan Inc. p. 40 right; Yerbury and Son p. 39.

Illustrations by Richard Hook, Andrew Howat and Mel Wright

Front cover illustration: 'Shipbuilding on the Clyde: Furnaces' by Stanley Spencer R. A. Courtesy of the Trustees of the Imperial War Museum.

Back cover: 'The Gorbals' by Bert Hardy/The Hulton Picture Company

The author would like to thank Mrs Olive Checkland and Professor Christopher Harvie for commenting on a draft of this book, and the School of Scottish Studies at the University of Edinburgh for access to material collected by the Scottish Labour History Society's Scottish Working People's Oral History Project. This project was funded by the Manpower Services Commission and the material is Crown copyright. Extracts included in this book are reproduced with the permission of the Controller of Her Majesty's Stationery Office.

CONTENTS

Workshop of the British Empire

By the end of the nineteenth century Scotland had become one of the world's wealthiest nations. Scottish products found eager buyers in many countries. And Scottish men and women could be found around the globe – as explorers or missionaries, soldiers, sailors, engineers, scientists, doctors, teachers, and farmers. So the world had come to know and respect the Scots and their achievements. By brain and brawn, Scotland had made herself the workshop of the British Empire.

Textile Towns

Cotton was an industry in decline by 1880. But three Scottish towns had found their own ways of making money out of textiles.

Jute was the speciality of Dundee.

Jute is a coarse fibre from the bark of a plant that grows in the Bengal area of East India, now the country of Bangladesh. It had been used there for centuries to make mats. Then a Dundee man discovered in the 1830's that if the jute was softened by whale-oil it could be woven by machine. Dundee had lots of whale-oil, for it was a whaling port. So the jute industry grew, and grew. The jute was used for anything from coal sacks to nose-bags for horses.

Right Jute, from raw material to finished products *Below* Work stops for a photograph inside a Dundee weaving shed, around 1900

By the 1880s there were over 70 jute mills and factories in Dundee. The biggest factory of all was the Camperdown works. Fourteen thousand people worked there. It was impossible to miss, because above it towered one of the biggest chimneys in Scotland: Cox's Stack, measuring 85 metres from top to bottom. People called Dundee 'Juteopolis', and for a while it had no rivals. Except in far-off Bengal, where jute mills were growing. Indeed, some of these Calcutta mills were owned by Dundee jutemasters, equipped with Scottish machinery. By the 1890s competition from Calcutta had become fierce, and Juteopolis was facing a slow decline.

Top An 1880 floor covering design from Nairn's of Kirkcaldy *Right* Cotton reel labels, some with the famous Anchor symbol *Above* Bobbins being made on scalloping machines in the Coats Mill, Paisley

Another Fife town, Kirkcaldy, created its place in the sun by concentrating on linoleum. Linoleum is a tough floor-covering, cheaper than carpet and hard-wearing. It is made by coating canvas with a layer of solid linseed oil, and had been invented in the 1860s. Kirkcaldy already had a floor-covering industry, making vast quantities of floor-cloth. But in 1877, Michael Nairn, Kirkcaldy's chief floor-cloth maker, started making linoleum. By the 1880s, Nairn's linoleum was well-known throughout Britain and indeed the world, with branches in the United States.

The third town to devote itself to textiles was Paisley. It already had a long tradition of weaving, and for a short time in the 1830s and 1840s had enjoyed a booming demand for its shawls. Paisley's new product was cotton thread, and the leading company was J & P Coats.

By the end of the century Coats mills could be found in many countries, from India to Russia. So they were one of the first 'multinationals': companies operating in several countries. Multinationals have been the most successful companies in the twentieth century.

In 1896 Coats combined with their four main competitors, including Clarks, and so controlled most of the world's thread industry. With the competition gone, Coats could for a time control thread prices, and huge profits were made. In fact eleven members of the Coats family became millionaires.

By the turn of the century 10,000 people worked in the giant Anchor and Ferguslie mills that straddled Paisley. But a visitor had only to look at the town's street names to know that Paisley's business was textiles: they included Cotton Street, Silk Street, Gauze Street, Lawn Street, Shuttle Street, Mill Street and, of course, Thread Street.

5

One reason for the success of thread-making was the spread of the sewing-machine. This American invention had first been seen in Britain in 1851, and in 1856 a German-American called Isaac Singer opened a shop in Buchanan Street, Glasgow. The machines were an instant success, and in 1867 Singer decided to start making machines in Glasgow. He started with a small plant in Love Loan, off High John Street, making 30 machines a week. Then he moved to a bigger factory in Bridgeton, making 3000 machines a week.

Still this was not enough to keep up with the demand. So in 1882 work began on an even bigger factory in Kilbowie in Clydebank. When it opened in 1885, it was the largest factory in Europe. It covered 19 hectares and made 10,000 sewing machines every week. It was a far cry from the cramped little workshop in Love Loan.

The picture shows a vast crowd of workers leaving the Singer factory in Clydebank. The railway station was named Singer after the company.

James Hunter, a weaver in one of the lace mills of Irvine Valley in Ayrshire, remembers how the piece rate system affected the weavers at their jacquard machines:

'They had tae be up and down the ladders behind their machine, up onto the Jacquards to change cards, reverse them and what have you. One o' the stories when ah started wis one o' the weavers had decided tae take a short cut comin' back down and jumped over the front o' the machine and had went over on his ankle. A couple o' men ran over to help him and he says, 'Don't bother with me', he says, 'get the machine on!'

The first week ah started I remember running past this machine and the weaver comin' after me, cursin' and swearin' – the draught o' me runnin' past him would knock his machine off and interfere wi' his wages!' He also remembers a game he used to play to annoy the older weavers: 'I would hide behind the machine and you could always watch the rhythm o' the machine and start whistling as if the machine wis squeaking. So the weaver would rush for his oil can and he would oil where he thought the squeak was comin' from. So I just stopped for a minute or two, moved along and started again and it wis guaranteed that he would rush for this oil can, there was no way this machine would get put off for the lack of oil – they always seemed to have an oil can in their hand, the weavers.'

So by the beginning of the twentieth century Scotland's textile industries employed many people. It was noisy work, surrounded by clattering machines. And in the cotton mills it was uncomfortable work, because the mills were kept hot and damp to prevent the thread from breaking. In some mills there was a 'piece rate' system that paid workers according to how much they produced. But two out of every three textile workers were women, and they were paid much less than men, even if the work they did was the same. In 1906 men in the cotton industry earned £1.54 per week, women only 63p.

Coal

Between 1880 and 1914 coal was a fast-growing industry. The amount of coal brought to the surface doubled to 40 million tonnes a year. 150,000 miners were at work in Scotland's mining areas. They stretched from Ayrshire through Lanarkshire and Dumbartonshire to Stirling, Lothian and Fife.

By 1900 Scotland's coal industry was shifting to the east, to the new coal-fields of Fife and Lothian. Much of the coal from these new fields was exported to eastern Europe and Russia, and the export trade gave a big boost to east coast ports. So Leith, Grangemouth, and Methil all grew in the early 1900s.

The miners relied on muscle, pick and shovel to dig the 'black gold'. Electric coal cutting machines were around from the 1880's onwards: in fact they had been invented by a Scottish company – Anderson, Boyes of Motherwell. But the Scottish mine owners were slow to make use of them, and by 1913 four tons in every five were still mined by hand.

Top A map of Scotland's coalfields around 1900 *Above* An artist's impression of coalmining in 1871

Mining was full of danger. The pits would flood, or collapse, or fill with poisonous gases. In 1877 an enormous explosion suddenly ripped through a pit in Blantyre, leaving 207 miners dead in one of Scotland's worst ever disasters. And the mining villages were dreadful places. The houses were usually damp, dark, crowded rows of cottages, where disease flourished. Conditions were worst in Lanarkshire, the oldest and biggest coalfield. The coal seams there were beginning to run out of coal, and the response of the owners was to keep costs down by cutting the miners' wages. They tried to set miner against miner. Irish, Polish and German miners were encouraged to come and work for less money. Religious differences were encouraged.

Too often, the 'divide and rule' tactics worked. In 1880 the Lanarkshire miners went on strike for six weeks but were forced back to work defeated. In 1881 the Ayrshire men were on strike for 10 weeks until they too were defeated. At Blantyre in 1887 strikers clashed fiercely with the police.

In the face of such defeats, the miners slowly forged a new weapon: the trade union. The union banners proclaimed their purpose – 'Unity is strength'. But unity was hard to achieve, trade unions were slow to spread. In 1912, miners in the Tarbrax Colliery near West Calder still did not have a strong trade union. Instead they rioted, wrecking the colliery and burning down the engine-house.

Oil . . . in 1900

Coal was not the only thing mined in Scotland. In Lothian a huge field of shale oil was discovered. This was oil that was suspended in slate-like rock, and it was the only big field in Europe outside Russia. A man from Bathgate called James Young discovered a way of squeezing the oil out of the shale, and 4000 men were working in the Lothian shalefield by the 1900s.

Iron and Steel

The iron mines of Scotland were close to exhaustion by 1900. But this did not hold back the ironmasters. With rich ores imported from countries like Spain, they started making the miracle material of the time – steel. Steel was so much stronger and better than iron that iron bridges and ships were scrapped and replaced with steel. Demand soared and the steel-making towns of Scotland grew like gold-rush towns. Airdrie, Coatbridge, Motherwell, Cambuslang, Gartcosh, Mossend and Wishaw all threw themselves into the new steel industry. In 1879 they produced just 50,000 tonnes, but by 1911 this had rocketed to one and one quarter *million* tonnes.

Beardmore

Steel is much stronger than iron, but this makes it much more difficult to work with.

Shale oil was valuable, but huge mounds of waste were created. They can be seen to this day, scarring the countryside. This photograph was taken near Bathgate.

Only one forge in Scotland proved equal to the task: the Parkhead Forge in the east end of Glasgow, owned by William Beardmore. In the 1880s Beardmore began to equip his forge with machines that could handle steel. First he bought a huge steam hammer to smash the steel into slabs ready for rolling. One of his

Massive machines are needed to pound and hammer steel into shape, to cut it, and bend it. Here, a propeller shaft is being forged in Beardmore's Parkhead Forge. The photograph was probably taken in 1914.

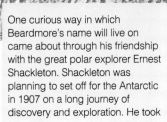

Top The Beardmore Glacier in Antarctica *Above* The Beardmore snow cat on Shackleton's Antarctic expedition. *Right* William Beardmore *Far Right* Ernest Shackleton

One curious way in which Beardmore's name will live on came about through his friendship with the great polar explorer Ernest Shackleton. Shackleton was planning to set off for the Antarctic in 1907 on a long journey of discovery and exploration. He took snow-cats with him, sledges and other equipment built or bought at Beardmore's. When Shackleton returned from the Antarctic in 1909, he announced that as a mark of gratitude he had named the huge glacier he had discovered the Beardmore Glacier.

workers, a man called David Kirkwood who would later become famous as a trade union leader, remembered that the hammer, called Samson, 'made the whole district around Parkhead quiver as in an earthquake'.

In 1888 Beardmore installed an even heavier hammer called Goliath. Then in 1896 work began on putting in a press so powerful that it could exert a force of 12000 tonnes. Beardmore used it to shape armour plating for the Royal Navy's latest battleships. Engineers came from around the world to learn from the Parkhead Forge. Japanese engineers came to learn how to make armour plate in the 1900s, and one story is that they copied so closely that from then on Japanese forges would fill with cries of 'Awa Parkhead' and 'Awa Camlachie' as the great plates were bent into shape!

The main reason for Beardmore's success was the success of Clyde shipbuilding. The Parkhead Forge had a constant stream of orders from the shipyards. It was one of the few places in the world that could make a steel propeller shaft over 20 metres long and dead straight to within thousandths of a centimetre. In fact shipbuilding was so important to Beardmore's that it opened its own shipbuilding yard at Dalmuir on the Clyde in 1902. By then, around 40 yards were on the river. They were the beating heart of Scotland during their heyday, which lasted from around 1870 to 1914.

Shipbuilding

In 1870 one of the most famous sailing ships of all time, the Cutty Sark, was launched at Dumbarton.

Scotland had played an important part in the era of sailing ships. The clipper yards of the Clyde, Dundee, Leith and Aberdeen had built high-class ships for the tea-trade with the Far East. Great rope and canvas works had grown in Greenock; Dundee and Arbroath had supplied most of the sails for the Royal Navy.

But the end of sail was in sight, and in the new era of steamships Scotland had a much larger role. Scottish engineers had pioneered new efficient marine steam engines and boilers. By 1876 three-quarters of British merchant ships were powered by their inventions. Then in 1879 another big breakthrough occurred: William Denny, a shipyard in Dumbarton, launched a ship called the *Rotomahana*. It was the first ocean-going ship in the world with a hull made of steel. Steel was stronger and meant that bigger, faster, more efficient ships could be built. The advantages of steel were so great that within 6 or 7 years of the *Rotomahana's* launch almost every yard on the Clyde had switched to steel.

Soon yards all along the Clyde were expanding to keep up with new orders from all over the world.

The process of building the ships was similar in all the yards. Everything was done in the open air, with no protection from the weather. On a slipway that sloped into the river, the builders would first lay the keel of the ship, and then the ribs that formed a steel skeleton. Then began the job of building the ship's skin, out of hundreds of plates each fixed to its neighbours by rivets. Riveting involved pushing a white hot pin of metal through holes on the edge of the plates, then bashing the ends flat so that the plates were held tightly together. It was work that often involved boys – the rivet boys whose job was to heat up the rivets and then toss them quickly into place to be hammered by a riveter. The noise was deafening, particularly in the cramped spaces inside the ship. Many a rivet boy had his ear drums split by the racket and lost his hearing early in life. With the hull complete the ship was launched into the river then floated to a fitting-out basin where everything was added to make a complete ship. Items of every shape and size arrived at the basin, from the boilers to the ship's compass and anchor chain. All of this created jobs for people all over Scotland. Finally, the ship was taken down river to the 'measured mile' off Skelmorlie, where she would be put through her paces under the watchful eyes of her builders and her new owners. Then papers were signed, handshakes exchanged, and another Clyde-built ship was ready for a life at sea.

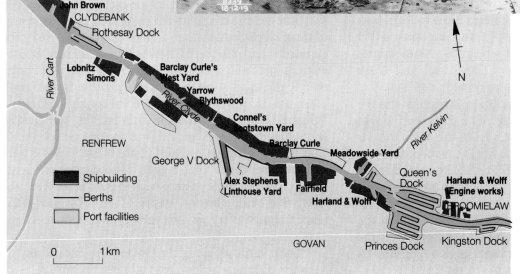

Top The Rotomahana, built in Dumbarton, the world's first ocean-going steel ship. *Above* Inside a ship being built early this century. All the girders have been carefully numbered. The man on the left seems to have a rolled-up plan by his feet. A young apprentice stands by. *Left* A map of the Clyde shipyards on the eve of the First World War *Opposite* A Dreadnought-type ship, the battle-cruiser HMS Indomitable

Clyde heyday

In the years from the 1870s up to the start of the Great War in 1914, almost one in five of the world's ships came from the Clyde. The annual tonnage of ships launched soared from 200,000 tonnes in 1870 to over 750,000 tonnes by 1913.

The quality of the ships improved enormously too. The journey across the Atlantic was slashed from 14 days to 7 by the *S.S. Arizona*, launched at Fairfield's yard in 1879. It became the holder of the Blue Riband, the coveted and glamorous prize for the fastest Atlantic crossing. The *Arizona* was followed by a whole series of 'Atlantic greyhounds' from the Clyde yards, each improving slightly on the record. But the Clyde's position could not last. First, other countries were catching up with the Clyde in shipbuilding methods. Germany showed what it could do in 1897, when the German liner *Kaiser Wilhelm Der Grosse* won the Blue Riband. Then in 1911 the first ship in the world with a diesel engine instead of a steam engine was launched in Copenhagen. The Clyde responded with a diesel ship the following year, but it was becoming clear that other countries were not just catching up: they were beginning to overtake the Clyde.

Diesel engines popped up early in the century in a story by Neil Munro, a popular writer who came from Inverary in Argyllshire but worked in Glasgow. His stories in the *Evening News* had a big following, especially those about a Clyde puffer called the *Vital Spark* and its crew of characters: Para Handy the captain, Macphail the engineer, and Dougie and Sunny Jim. Let's go on board for a few minutes:

'A motor-boat regatta was going on at Dunoon; the *Vital Spark* seemed hardly to be moving as some of the competitors flashed past, breathing petrol fumes.

'You canna do anything like that', said Dougie to the engineer, who snorted.

'No', said Macphail contemptuously, 'I'm an engineer; I never was much o' a hand at the sewin' machine. I couldna' lower mysel' to handle engines ye could put in your waistcoat pocket.'

'Whether you would or no'', said Para Handy, 'the times iss changin', and the motor-launch iss coming for to stop.'

'That's whit she's aye daein',' retorted the engineer; 'stoppin's her strong p'int; gie me a good substantial compound engine; nane o' your hurdy-gurdies.'

In one area, however, the yards were going from strength to strength. This was in work for the Royal Navy. In the 1880s Germany had begun to flex its new industrial muscles, and build its own Navy to serve its growing empire. Work began on a new powerful German battle fleet. Britain responded in 1905 by ordering a new kind of battleship, the *Dreadnought*. Then Germany started work in 1907 on its own dreadnought-type battleships. In 1909 Britain responded again by ordering 'super-dreadnoughts'.

This arms race brought lots of work to the Clyde yards, and ended a very bad slump in 1906. But the bonanza was temporary: by 1914 the race to build battleships had turned into war between Britain and Germany. The arms race had become a death race.

Work to do . . .

1 **a** What three towns specialised in: thread; jute; linoleum?
  b What was the 'piece rate' system? Describe in your own words the effect it had on the weavers in the lace mills. Why did it have that effect?
2 Which Scottish coal ports were growing around 1900? Why was it an advantage for them to be on the east coast?
3 Explain in your own words what is meant by 'divide and rule' tactics. In what ways did Scotland's coal-mine owners try to use these tactics? How did the miners try to resist the owners?
4 How did the Beardmore Glacier in Antarctica get its name? What were 'Samson' and 'Goliath' in the Parkhead Forge? Why did they have to be so powerful?
5 Study the picture of the men building a ship. Then describe what you see and the stage the ship has reached.

At Home and Going Out

Home Life

What were people's homes like at the beginning of this century?

James Glendenning was born in Laurie Street, Leith, in 1905. This is how he remembers his home:

'. . . it was four storey tenements and I stayed on the top flat. In each of these tenements on each of the four storeys, there were four houses, and in each flat was one toilet which was divided among the four families . . . The houses composed o' a but and ben, a room and a kitchen. The kitchens were say about ten feet square, with a bed recess on one side of it and the bed was built in, a wooden structure built into the bed recess, which they used to put at that time it was a flock mattress. There was no spring mattresses in those days. It was simply a bag filled with flocks (tufts of wool) laid on top of the boards. And on the other side of the room was a window. Under the window was the sink. No hot water of course, it was simply cold water, and at one side of the sink was what we called the bunker. It was a cupboard affair, the lid lifted and it held about a hundredweight of coal. And that's where they kept the coal. Now all the cooking, all the heating was by the fire, which was a large black leaded grate maybe four feet high, and everything was done on that. As far as the washing was concerned, the women had to wash in the middle of the floor. They had a large pan, it was more like a bath with a handle over the top, that was hooked on to a crook that was an iron contraption that hung over the top of the fire and it heated the water. Now the washing was done as I say, in a tub, on a small stool, the tub was placed on a small stool and the women rubbed them with a scrubbing board, and cleaned them in that way. And to dry them they used to have a line to the building opposite on a pulley, and they used to pin clothes on one of the double ropes, and pull the other one until it was out to where they wanted, that was their method of drying.'

James Glendenning's house in Leith was typical of Scotland's industrial towns and cities.

In 1911 half of the population lived in one or two-roomed houses. This was much worse than in England at that time: south of the border, only one in twelve people lived in such small houses.

Things were especially bad in Glasgow. There, many people would have found even a room and kitchen spacious, for they had only one room. In this 'single end', everything had to be done in the same room – washing, cooking, eating, sitting and sleeping. There was no space to play, and no spare corner to huff or sulk in.

Electricity was slow to catch on in Scotland. In Glasgow in 1901 there were only 3000 homes with a supply. Paraffin lamps had been normal to light homes until the 1890s, but they were smoky and dim, and there was always the danger that they might start a fire. Then in the 1890s the coin-in-the-slot gas meter was invented, and houses could begin to use gas lights. Early gas lights were just a jet of burning gas, but by the turn of the century people were using gas 'mantles', a special fabric that glowed brightly when burning gas flowed over it.

And a gas supply led to another new household appliance: the gas cooker. This transformed the lives of women at home. Instead of spending an hour or more each day in the dirty and heavy work of lighting, stoking and cleaning the range, cooking could be done at the turn of a knob. In 1898 only one in 14 houses in Glasgow had a gas cooker, but more than half had them by 1914.

Between 1841 and 1911 Glasgow grew from 275,000 to 784,000 people, Edinburgh from 164,000 to 401,000, Aberdeen from 65,000 to 164,000, Dundee from 60,000 to 165,000. Some smaller places like Airdrie, Coatbridge and Clydebank changed from villages to towns in just a few years. So houses were just thrown up.

Part of the reason for the bad housing was that the towns and cities had grown so quickly.

Another reason was that the wages of most people who worked were very low. A one-roomed tenement flat at least kept down the heating bills and the rent.

Above An advert for gas lighting, from around 1900
Below The growth of Scotland's cities

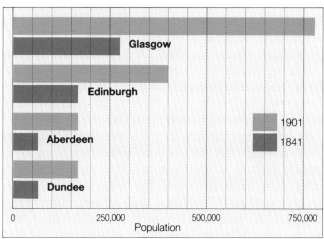

13

Disease

Slum children in old photographs often have badly bent legs. This is a sign of a disease called rickets, where the body's bones are not getting enough vitamin D, and become soft. It is caused by a diet like this, described in the year 1886: 'A loaf of bread is taken from the shelf: an old brown teapot gets a spoonful of tea and is filled with boiling water from a rusty kettle on the hob; a lump of salt butter, wrapped in a piece of dirty paper, is produced, or a little jelly or syrup; two of three broken cups are put on a rickety chair, round which the children cluster, either on stools or squatted on the floor, or on the edge of the iron fender. Sugar is cheap; milk a rare commodity; if the earnings of the family can afford it some ham is boiled; and so, without any kind of order and with a general scramble, they all fall to and quickly consume what is provided for them. This constitutes the principle meal of thousands of poor children, day after day. Tea without milk and bread without butter is very usual fare.'

Slums were cheap to build and cheap to rent, but their cost in terms of human life was terribly high. The damp and crowded conditions were perfect for diseases to flourish. Especially bad were the infectious diseases affecting the chest and lungs, diseases like tuberculosis, bronchitis and pneumonia. These diseases were the mass killers that children and young adults were especially likely to catch. And when death came?

'Their little bodies are laid on a table or on a dresser so as to be somewhat out of the way of their brothers and sisters, who play and sleep and eat in their ghastly company. From beginning to rapid-ending the lives of these children are short . . . one in every five of all who are born there never see the end of their first year.'

These are the words of Dr J. B. Russell. He was Glasgow's Medical Officer of Health between 1872 and 1898, and a child's death in a crowded one-room slum house was a common sight for him. Scottish cities had started to appoint these Medical Officers in the 1860s: Edinburgh had the first in 1862. But the best of them soon realised that there was no point in waiting until people became ill and then trying to cure them with medicines that didn't work. Far better to stop diseases from spreading by tackling their causes: dirty water supplies, no proper toilets or sewers, dirty food, bad housing, bad diets and low incomes. Water was the first

Top Dundee children around 1910 *Above* A family gravestone, Edinburgh

thing to be cleaned up. Glasgow's supply from Loch Katrine was so successful in reducing diseases that other towns were quick to follow. Edinburgh piped in a supply from Talla Reservoir in the Borders, Dundee from Loch of Lintrathen in Angus, and so on. By 1900 most Scottish towns had their own clean water supply.

Next came the huge job of building a proper sewage system. This meant laying hundreds of miles of pipes and tunnels under the towns and cities. Then the waste had to be filtered and cleaned at sewage 'farms', and not just poured into the nearest river or sea. It was very expensive, but by 1890 Glasgow had 100 miles of sewer running under the streets, making the city safer, healthier and less smelly. And by 1910 the Clyde was a bit cleaner too, with big sewage farms at Dalmarnock, Dalmuir and Shieldhall.

Clearing the slums

Housing, too, was gradually getting a bit better. Aberdeen's main slum area, Shorelands, was cleaned up in the 1870s and 1880s. In Edinburgh the slums around the Cowgate and Chambers Street were torn down to make way for new buildings. By the 1890s Glasgow's worst slums were confined to a few definite areas around Calton, Cowcaddens and the Gorbals.

Of course there was no point in clearing slums if new houses were not built for the people who had stayed in them. A few co-operatives were started, where people joined together to build their own houses. In Edinburgh, for instance, the stone masons formed their own Co-operative Building Society and built cottages in Stockbridge. But most of the building right up to 1914 was done by small private builders, often working on just three or four houses at a time. Their standards rose too, as government regulations laid down more rules about bigger windows, better plumbing, more space.

Building the sewers: a modern impression

Many of the people who campaigned most strongly for better health and housing came from the middle and upper classes. Some were doctors. Others raised money for charitable purposes. A good example was William Quarrier, who started a village home for Glasgow orphans in the countryside near Kilmacolm. Many schools, hospitals, homes and halls were built by this kind of effort.

But most people with money found another way of coping with the slums: they moved farther and farther away from them.

By the early twentieth century every Scottish city and town had its own middle class housing areas, of solid villas and semi-villas and clean leafy streets. In Aberdeen it was to the west, around Queen's Cross (pictured left), and outwards. In Dundee, Broughty Ferry was like a different world compared with the cramped slums of Lochee. Edinburgh already had the Georgian elegance of the new town; next, solid Victorian villas were laid out in Merchiston and Morningside. In Glasgow the middle classes moved westwards to Kelvinside and along the Great Western Road. They also moved south to Cathcart, Pollockshields, Queen's Park and Giffnock. A few people with enough money moved right out of the city, to Helensburgh or Troon or Bridge of Weir. From there, they could commute by train or steamer to and from work.

15

Shopping

Above Sir Thomas Lipton *Right* Advert for Lipton's Tea, 1896

Tea was becoming more and more popular in the 1880's, but it was usually sold loose in shops. Customers could not be sure that they were getting the amount they had paid for. The quality also varied, and it was quite common for used tea leaves to be gathered, dried out and dyed, and then sold again to innocent shoppers. Lipton sold his tea in packets of a standard weight and quality, so people knew they were not being cheated.

Towards the end of the nineteenth century a modern shopping industry began to appear in Scotland, offering low prices and high quality. The most famous of the new shopkeepers was Thomas Lipton.

Thomas Lipton was born in Glasgow in 1850. When he left school he was only nine years old, but he found work and had soon saved enough to buy a ticket on a liner to New York.

In New York he got a job in a grocery store. Three years later, still a teenager, he was back in Glasgow bursting with the new ideas he had seen in the New York shops. When he opened his own shop in 1870, he began to try these ideas out.

Within a few years new Lipton's shops were opening all over Scotland, at the rate of one a week. England came next, and by 1885 more than 600 Lipton shops were busily trading.

At first, Lipton shops sold mainly hams, eggs, cheese and butter. Next, Lipton entered the tea market, and again with dramatic success.

Lipton became a very wealthy man as a result of his business successes. Later in his life he was well-known for his love of sailing and for the beautifully made yachts, always called *Shamrock*, that he bought and raced in Britain and America. But when he died in 1931 he was still known best for the great changes he had brought to shopping.

Another great force for change in Scotland's shops was the Co-operative Movement. Co-operatives were societies of shoppers, who got together to run their own shops. That way, they could make sure they weren't diddled or sold rubbish. And the profits of the Co-op shops were passed back to the shoppers: the more you spent, the more you got back.

By 1900, Co-operative shops could be found all over Scotland, and one in every ten Scots was a member of a Co-op society. And Co-op factories had sprung up to supply the shops with bread and biscuits, shirts and socks, pickles and boots, coffee and carpets.

COMING FROM LIPTON   GOING TO LIPTON

ONE OF THE EARLIEST LIPTON ADVERTISEMENTS WHICH WERE DISPLAYED IN THE WINDOWS OF HIS SHOPS. THESE CRUDE BUT LAUGHABLE CARTOONS WERE ALTERED WEEK BY WEEK AND PEOPLE FLOCKED FROM ALL OVER GLASGOW TO SEE THEM

Lipton had noticed in America that all the firms who were doing well were advertising their wares, in newspapers, posters and elsewhere. So he started to advertise his ham shop in Stobcross Street, Glasgow. He would buy the fattest, finest pigs he could find at the meat market, have them scrubbed and polished, then herd them through the streets of Glasgow to his shop. The pigs would have blue and pink ribbons round their necks and painted on their sides the words: 'I'm going to Lipton's. The best shop in town for Irish bacon!' Soon the name Lipton was on everyone's lips, and more and more customers were coming to the shop. Another idea was to have a line of very thin men walking up one side of the street holding signs saying 'Going to Lipton's' and another line of fat and jolly-looking men walking down the other side of the street 'Coming from Lipton's!'

School

A new Scottish school system came into being in 1872, and was to last right up until the First World War. The main idea was to take the schools away from the parishes that had been running them, and hand them over to elected School Boards. Children had to attend school from the age of 5 until they were 13. If their parents couldn't afford to send them to school they would get help. If any area did not have a decent school then one would be built.

It was a good system, and stopped Scotland from slipping behind other countries. It ensured that everyone was taught the basic skills of social life, especially the oddly named 'three R's': reading, writing, and 'rithmetic. And it was gradually improved even more. In 1883 the leaving age was raised to 14. New subjects were introduced, like domestic science in 1897 as a way of improving the Scottish diet. By 1900 all fees had been abolished, making education a right. By 1908 the number of children at school had doubled to one million, while the school buildings were much more numerous and handsome. And although very few people got the chance to go on to university, the chance of doing so was better than in England or elsewhere in Europe. All in all, there was a lot to be proud of in the Scottish education system.

But there were problems too. So many new children were being sent to school that classrooms became crowded: one description told of a class of 70 with the teacher shouting at them like a drover shouting at his sheep! The crowding and shortage of money meant that the schools became a bit like factories churning out tinned peas.

Technical subjects and science were not encouraged. This made it very difficult for Scotland to keep up with other countries like Germany, Japan and America, where these subjects were seen as very important.

On top of these problems, some people complained that there was too much English influence, and that in subjects like history the schools taught too much about England and not enough about Scotland. These complaints were especially strong from the Gaelic organisation An Comunn Gaidhealach. They claimed that the Gaelic language was being killed because the schools didn't teach it. But the problem was that many Highlanders wanted their children to be taught in English. They thought that being educated in English would make it easier for their children to get on in the world. As a school inspector said in 1899, 'the language is beautiful . . . but the people do not want it.'

Some people at the time were well aware of the problems in Scottish schools. One was a young teacher called A. S. Neill, who was working in a village school just before the First World War:

'Tonight, after my bairns had gone away, I sat down on a desk and thought, What does it all mean? What am I trying to do? These boys are going out to the fields to plough; these girls are going to farms as servants . . . I can teach them to read, and they will read serials in the drivelling weeklies, I can teach them to write, and they will write pathetic notes to me bye and bye; I can teach them to count, and they will never count more than the miserable sum they receive as a weekly wage . . . My work is hopeless, for education should aim at bringing up a new generation that will be better than the old. The present system is to produce the same kind of man as we see today.'

But his ideas on how to improve things were given more attention abroad than in his home country.

Schoolgirls, mainly thirteen and fourteen years old, at class in Scotland Street School, Glasgow, 1916. Discipline and drilling were strict, with lots of competition and frequent use of the strap or tawse as punishment. Stinging hands became a painfully familiar memory of school.

Church on Sunday

Religion held an important place in nineteenth-century Scotland. Almost all marriages took place in church. Up to one third of all Scots went to morning service. Many more listened carefully to the views of church leaders on the great issues of the day. Some people even claimed that the annual gathering of the Church of Scotland in Edinburgh – the General Assembly – was the nearest thing to a Scottish Parliament.

The Church did not speak with one voice. The protestant Church of Scotland had argued with other protestants, who had formed their own 'Free' church. And immigration from Ireland had greatly increased the number of Roman Catholic Scots.

Disputes between churches were fierce and bitter. The Free Church, for instance, accused the Church of Scotland of running 'synagogues of Satan'. But by 1900 the churches were coming to see that these disputes won them few friends or converts. So they began to draw closer together, and made fresh efforts to spread their gospel of Christianity. Abroad, Scottish churches expanded their missionary efforts. And at home, the churches tried to do more to ease social problems such as homelessness, poverty, and alcoholism.

Drink

Drink was the cause of many problems. Drink was cheap, and there seemed to be a pub on every street corner. The Scottish pubs were grim, dark places. Men went to get drunk while women usually stayed away.

Many men became seriously ill and died young. The police were kept busy by the violence and disorder

A pledge card with the signature Tom Honeyman, signed in 1883

it caused. The worst type of violence was to frightened wives and terrified children.

Some church members started groups called Temperance Societies to fight against drunkenness. The Glasgow publisher William Collins printed millions of leaflets advertising these societies. One temperance society was called the Independent Order of Good Templars. It started in 1869 and within 7 years had 1100 branches in Scotland. Another society was called the Band of Hope. Then in 1879 the Salvation Army moved to Scotland and began to campaign against drink. It urged people to give up drink and become 'tee-total' by 'signing the pledge' that they would never drink alcohol. Trade Unionists also preached the dangers of drink, and many Labour leaders, like Keir Hardie, decided that 'tee-total' was the best policy.

Two lantern slides from around 1900. One warns of the dangers of drink, the other shows the rewards of temperance.

Boys Brigade

In 1869 a man called William Alexander Smith arrived in Glasgow. He too was a churchman and part of the temperance movement. He wanted to give boys something to do with their time, something to keep them out of trouble and away from the pub. In North Woodside he started a new kind of Christian Sunday school where boys over 12 were taught to march, drill, do exercises, and play team games. In 1883 this became the Boys Brigade, and quickly spread through Scotland. Now there are over 80,000 boys in Britain in the Boys Brigade, plus another 20,000 in more than thirty other countries.

Above The modern Boys Brigade *Below* Amateur football in South Side Park, Glasgow in 1890. Big crowds, bad tempers, lots of free advice.

Sporting Scotland

The end of the nineteenth century also saw a big increase in sport. Cycling, rugby, cricket, tennis, golf and boxing all flourished. But for most Scottish men, sport meant only one thing: football. Modern rules for the game were agreed in London in 1863 and in 1867 Scotland's first club was formed – Queen's Park. By 1890, 11 teams were organised into a league, and the players were no longer amateurs playing for nothing, but professionals getting paid to play.

Spectators crowded through the turnstiles to watch 'ra gemme', and the grounds became larger and larger. Within thirty years the Queen's Park football club had knocked down and rebuilt their Hampden Park stadium three times. By 1914 it was the first ground in the world able to hold more than 100,000 people. And supporter's trains, which the railways started to run in the 1890s, allowed fans to follow their teams around the country.

Hey-day of the Clyde steamers. Crowds on the quay and crowds aboard as the *Benmore* leaves the Broomielaw. At the start of the Fair Holiday the Broomielaw was pandemonium, with crowds of people, luggage, carts, horses and boats all jostling for space.

All over Britain, towns and villages had for centuries had special days each year when a fair would be held, or when a holy day was celebrated. By the end of the nineteenth century, fair days had become the 'fair' weekends and holy days had become 'holidays'. They were a chance to escape from the dirt and grime of town and city, and head for the country or the seaside. Trains, trams and steamships now made holidays possible for almost everyone, and soon special holiday resorts grew up around the coast. For people from Edinburgh, the nearest resort was Portobello. Like all the best resorts it had a long promenade built along the sea front, and a pier with amusements. Holidaymakers could take donkey rides along the beach, or catch a steamer across the Forth to Fife. The more daring could swim in the sea. This involved changing into a bathing costume in a hut mounted on wheels called a bathing machine. The hut was then pushed to the water edge, and the bather could jump into the sea.

The biggest holiday resorts were all on the Clyde. Dunoon, Rothesay, Brodick, Largs, Millport and Troon were reached by a steamer, and the journey came to be known as taking a trip 'doon the watter'. The most popular starting place was the Broomielaw in the centre of Glasgow.

The steamers were things of great beauty, full of polished wood and shining brass, with paddles on either side thrashing the water into a bubbling foam.

Competition between the different companies was fierce. Once two paddlers called the *Jupiter* and the *Waverley* were racing from Dunoon to Inellan, when the *Jupiter* suddenly veered hard to port and knocked the *Waverley* onto the beach!

By 1914, the Clyde steamers plied all over the Clyde estuary and beyond: to Arrochar, Ardrishaig, Tarbert and Campbeltown. Some of the boats could take many hundreds of passengers. The *Duchess of Hamilton* could carry 1900 people, the *Marchioness of Graham* 1500. So when the steamers arrived and holidaymakers poured off, it suddenly seemed as if Rothesay or Dunoon had become a mini-Glasgow, full of city voices and bustle.

A Good Night Out

Before 1914 the best place to go for a good night out was the music hall. They were noisy, smoky, and crowded. On stage you could see singing, juggling, performing dogs, conjuring, wild animals, comedy, and almost everything else. Every Scottish city had its music halls. Some were built with no expense spared, like the King's Theatre in Bath Street, Glasgow. When it opened in 1904 it was one of the best theatres in Britain, seating 2000 people in great luxury.

The music hall made some big stars, and one of the biggest was a Scotsman called Harry Lauder (pictured above with his wife in 1900). He came from Portobello near Edinburgh. His first public appearance was at a meeting organised by the Band of Hope, who encouraged music hall as another way of keeping people away from pubs. In 1900 he was a hit in London with a comedy act that the English loved. He wore a kilt and carried a crooked stick, and pretended to be very mean. When he went to the United States the Americans loved the act too. And no-one could draw a bigger crowd in Scotland. Some of the songs he sang are still well-known. They include *I Love a Lassie*, which he first sang in the pantomime Aladdin in Glasgow in 1905, and *Roamin' in the Gloamin'*, first sung in another Glasgow pantomime in 1910.

Music hall was still going strong in 1914, but there was a cuckoo in its nest. In 1896 the first flickering moving pictures were shown in public by the French Lumiere Brothers. Soon music halls were showing films of horse-racing or football matches. In 1905 a popular film, and one of the first British feature films, was a comedy about a Scotsman called McNab visiting his cousins in London. Music hall audiences were in fits of laughter at McNab, the country bumpkin. He is shown practising golf in the living room, then he terrifies the maid when his kilt falls off, and finally he is ordered back to Scotland in disgrace. Films like *McNab's Visit to London* were so popular that by 1908 the first cinema had appeared, showing nothing but movies. In a few more years the music hall would be a thing of the past.

Work to do . . .

1 Explain what is meant by: a but and ben; a gas mantle; a single end; a tenement.
2 What diseases were young people most likely to die from in the late nineteenth century? What were the main causes of these diseases? What was done to improve things?
3 Look at the advert for Lipton's Teas. Describe what is happening in the pictures in the advert. What does the advert tell you about the price, quality and popularity of Lipton's Tea?
4 List the changes made to improve Scottish schools between 1872 and 1914. Then write two short paragraphs saying what was **a** good, and **b** bad about Scotland's schools after these changes.
5 Study the two lantern slides showing temperance and drunkenness. Then make a list of the differences between the two households.
6 Why did Scottish churches worry about drink in the nineteenth century? What did they do about it?
7 Imagine a visit to the music hall around 1910. Write ten lines describing the atmosphere and the acts appearing on stage.

Getting About

Divers searching at the scene of the Tay Bridge Disaster.

The Railways

- Great North of Scotland Rlwy.
- Highland Railway
- North British Railway
- Caledonian Railway
- Dundee & Arbroath Joint Rlwy.
- Glasgow & South Western Rlwy.
- Portpatrick & Wigton Joint Rlwy.
- English Railways

0 25 50 km

N

Thurso
Wick
Helmsdale
Bonar Bridge
Elgin
Fraserburgh
Dingwall
Inverurie
Strome Ferry
Inverness
Kyle of Lochalsh
Fort Augustus
Aviemore
Aberdeen
Mallaig
Ballater
Fort William
Blair Atholl
Ballachulish
Montrose
Dunkeld
Arbroath
Oban
Crianlarich
Perth
Dundee
Crieff
St. Andrews
Stirling
Thornton Junction
Edinburgh
Gourock
Glasgow
Paisley
Berwick
Kilmarnock
Carstairs
Peebles
Ayr
Hawick
Girvan
Morpeth
Dumfries
Stranraer
Newcastle
Portpatrick
Kirkudbright
Carlisle

Four different lines snaked southwards to join the English network. Other lines pushed up through the Highlands to Thurso and Wick in the far north.

By 1880, Scotland's railway network was almost complete. Forty years of railway mania had created dozens of lines criss-crossing the central lowlands, linking mines, factories, ports and towns.

The impact of the railways was immense. Nothing was allowed to stand in their way. In Glasgow, the Caledonian Railway wanted a station right in the middle of the city for its English service. So in the 1870s it built a bridge over the river and just knocked down everything in its path to make way for the tracks. When it got to the heart of the city it built Central Station. In Edinburgh, too, the railway swept into the middle of the city. The North British Railway Company had to tunnel around the base of the Castle rocks and drain away a great lagoon of smelly water that stood in its way. That dried out lagoon is now Princes Street gardens!

Competition between the railway companies could be fierce, and produced disasters, triumphs and exciting races.

Disaster

The North British had pushed north from Edinburgh to Aberdeen, and had hired the engineer Thomas Bouch to build bridges over the Tay and Forth estuaries. Work on Bouch's Tay Bridge was finished by 1878. The bridge was over 3 kilometres long, and crossed the river in 86 spans over 27 metres above the water.

On December 28th 1879, as wild and stormy weather buffeted Scotland, Bouch and his family were sitting in their home in Edinburgh. Then a telegram arrived, with an appalling message:

> TERRIBLE ACCIDENT ON BRIDGE ONE OR MORE OF HIGH GIRDERS BLOWN DOWN STOP AM NOT SURE OF THE SAFETY OF THE LAST DOWN EDINBR TRAIN WILL ADVISE FURTHER AS SOON AS CAN BE OBTAINED STOP

As daylight broke on the Tay, a chilling sight was revealed. A whole section of the bridge had collapsed into the swirling estuary, taking with it the northbound mail train and killing all 79 passengers on board. As news of the Tay Bridge disaster was flashed by cable around the world, Parliament ordered an inquiry.

The report of the inquiry made sad reading. It found that the design of the bridge had been faulty, that poor materials had been used, that there had been bad workmanship and bad maintenance. Thomas Bouch's reputation and career were in ruins, and he died a broken man the following year.

The bridge had to be replaced, and by 1887 the second Tay Bridge was ready, the longest bridge in Britain's railway system. It runs alongside the remains of the old structure, whose piers can still be seen sticking out of the water, a favourite resting place for cormorants and other sea birds.

Triumph

The Forth Bridge leaps over the waters of the estuary in two huge arches each over half a kilometre long. Enough room had to be left under the bridge to let the tallest of tall ships through, so each arch is more than 45 metres above the surface of the Forth. No risks could be taken with safety, so the whole thing was built of steel rather than the weaker iron that had gone into the Tay Bridge.

With Bouch's Tay Bridge at the bottom of the river, it was clear that his Forth Bridge project would have to be abandoned. The railway companies turned instead to two engineers, John Fowler and Benjamin Baker. Both men were well used to working on a grand scale, and many of the projects they designed around the world – for instance, London's Metropolitan Underground railway – are still in daily use. 'The engineers, with their gigantic works, sweep everything before them in this Victorian era' said Baker, but their Forth Bridge plan was gigantic and spectacular even by Victorian standards.

Very few bridge builders in the world could have built the bridge, but one who could was the Glasgow firm of Tancred Arrol and Co. In December 1882 they were given the contract for the great task.

For six years work proceeded. Over 4600 men were brought together to assemble the great structure, one-third each from Scotland, England and Ireland. It was well-paid work, but it was also dangerous, and before the bridge was finished 57 men had been killed.

Finally, on March 4th 1890 the Prince of Wales was invited to drive home the last rivet on the bridge (the seven millionth!) and declare it open.

Fowler, Baker and Arrol all went on to honour, fame and fortune. Arrol's next big job was the Tower Bridge in London, Baker's the first Aswan Dam on the River Nile in Egypt. But the Forth Bridge remains the greatest monument to them and the men who built it. It is a Scottish wonder of the world.

A human cantilever in 1887 shows the principle behind the Forth Bridge. The man in the middle was a Japanese engineer studying Western skills.

A Caledonian Railway engine races past the winning post of Kinnaber Junction with the West Coast express, leaving its defeated East Coast rival to follow it the last few miles to Aberdeen. The painting is by Jack Hill.

With the Tay and Forth bridges in place, the east and west coast routes from London to Aberdeen began competing for passengers, and in 1895 a race to the north began.

Soon crowds were gathering at the London stations to watch the evening expresses set off. Newspapermen travelled back and forward to Aberdeen writing sensational accounts of the 'flyers' and 'racers' as speeds went up and up. At Berwick one night a crowd had gathered to watch the express pass through, knowing that trains were not meant to do more than 8 kilometres an hour on their way through the station. When they saw the express thundering towards them, hell for leather over the Royal Border Bridge at nearer to 100 kilometres an hour, they turned and ran for their lives!

Finally, on 22 August, 1895, the Euston express arrived in Aberdeen at 4.32 am, more than three hours faster than the same journey 5 weeks previously. Not until 200 kilometres per hour diesel trains were introduced in the 1970s was that record London-Aberdeen run of 8½ hours broken.

Motor Cars

By the turn of the century the railways were faced with a completely new competitor: the motor car. And although few people realised it at the time, the motor car would shape twentieth-century Scotland as much as the railways had shaped nineteenth-century Scotland.

The breakthrough happened in the 1880s, in Germany. It was another early sign that Scottish and English science and engineering was slipping behind. Gottleib Daimler and Karl Benz succeeded in designing an engine that ran on petrol. The petrol was squirted in tiny amounts into cylinders and then ignited by a spark. It exploded and forced pistons to move, driving the car. It was called an internal combustion engine, and modern car engines, although much more advanced, are direct descendents of Daimler and Benz's invention.

Soon Daimler and Benz and other Germans and French had started companies to make cars, and a few began to appear in Britain. At first they were only allowed to go at 5 kilometres an hour and someone had to walk in front of them warning people by waving a red flag. When the law was changed in 1896, several Scottish companies were quick to start making them. At first, the Scottish car-makers did quite well. But when the American Henry Ford showed the rest of the world how to mass-produce cars that were light and cheap, the Scottish car industry failed to adapt.

In 1900 the Argyll Company based in Bridgeton in Glasgow made Scotland's first car, called the *Voiturette* (voiture is French for car). It had a top speed of 30 kilometres an hour and cost £155, which was very expensive at the time. Another company was Arrol-Johnston, which started in Glasgow, then moved to Paisley, and finally to Dumfries. Albion was yet another Glasgow company.

The Argyll car did well at races on the famous Brooklands Track outside London in 1913, and for a short time Argyll claimed to be one of the largest makers of private cars in Europe. But all the Scottish cars tended to be heavy: the Arrol Johnston weighed three tons, which is twice the weight of many modern cars. Only Albion in Glasgow survived, by making trucks instead of cars.

Motoring in the early days was a great adventure. There were hardly any petrol stations, particularly north of Aberdeen, and motorists touring in these remote areas had to have petrol sent to them by railway! The roads were full of bumps and holes. In 1897 there had only been about 100 cars in the whole of Scotland, and in 1901 when a Mr J. H. Turner drove from Paisley to Langwell in Caithness – a journey of 480 kilometres that took three days – he met not a single motor car the whole way. But by 1914 there were nearer to 10,000 cars.

Of course, not everyone liked motor-cars. To begin with they were unreliable. They were also noisy and gave off fumes. They would startle horses, knock down pedestrians, and shake their passengers into a daze. Soon they were causing traffic jams and their owners were arguing for better roads, for parking spaces, for buildings to be knocked down to make way for them. But they also held out the attraction of speed, of excitement, of glamour, and of the freedom of the open road, and so while some people hated them others fell in love with them.

A pioneering motorist on a Highland road at the turn of the century

'. . . and with a blast of wind and a whirl of sound that made them jump for the nearest ditch, it was on them!'

In 1908 the Scottish writer Kenneth Grahame wrote a book called *The Wind in the Willows*. One of the many famous scenes in it describes the impact of the new-fangled motor car like this:

Mole, Toad and Water Rat are walking slowly along the country road behind their old grey horse and brightly-painted cart: '. . . when far behind them they heard a faint warning hum, like the drone of a distant bee. Glancing back, they saw a small cloud of dust, with a dark centre of energy, advancing on them at incredible speed, while from out of the dust a faint 'Poop-poop!' wailed like an uneasy animal in pain. Hardly regarding it, they turned to resume their conversation, when in an instant (as it seemed) the peaceful scene was changed, and with a blast of wind and a whirl of sound that made them jump for the nearest ditch, it was on them! The 'poop-poop' rang with a brazen shout in their ears, they had a moment's glimpse of an interior of glittering plate-glass and rich morocco, and the magnificent motor car, immense, breath-snatching, passionate, with its pilot tense and hugging his wheel, possessed all earth and air for the fraction of a second, flung an enveloping cloud of dust that blinded and en-wrapped them utterly, and then dwindled to a speck in the far distance, changed back into a droning bee once more.

The old grey horse, dreaming, as he plodded along, of his quiet paddock, in a new raw situation such as this simply abandonded himself to his natural emotions. Rearing, plunging, backing steadily, in spite of all the Mole's efforts at his head, and all the Mole's lively language directed at his better feelings, he drove the cart backwards towards the deep ditch at the side of the road. It paused an instant – then there was a heart-rending crash – and the canary-coloured cart, their pride and their joy, lay on its side in the ditch, an irredeemable wreck.

The Rat danced up and down in the road, simply transported with passion. 'You villains!' he shouted, shaking both fists, 'You scoundrels, you highwaymen, you-you-road hogs! – I'll have the law on you! I'll report you! I'll take you through all the Courts! . . .'

'Glorious, stirring sight!' murmured Toad, never offering to move. 'The poetry of motion! The *real* way to travel! The *only* way to travel! Here today – in next week tomorrow! Villages skipped, towns and cities jumped – always somebody else's horizon! O bliss! O poop-poop! O my! O my!'

Bicycles

Two penny-farthings and six safety bicycles, as the Newton of Barr, Tollhouse and Lochwinnoch Cycling Club goes on an outing in 1905

Only the rich could afford the first motor cars; bicycles were a different story. The 1870s saw the spread of 'penny-farthings': bicycles with one very big front wheel and a tiny rear wheel. The rider perched on top of the biggest wheel and wobbled off down bumpy roads, with an anxious and worried expression that became known as 'bicyclist's face'. The early machines had no brakes, and so the cyclist had to stop by choosing a soft grassy bank and then leaping off the bicycle while it was still going!

Then in the 1880s a different sort of bicycle appeared, called a 'safety' bicycle. It had two wheels of the same size, and was safer, cheaper and much easier to ride. 'Pneumatic' or air-filled rubber tyres, an invention that owed a great deal to the Scotsman James Dunlop, were added to these safety bicycles in the 1890s. A boom started in bicycle sales. Tens of thousands were made every year, and cycling clubs sprang up all over Scotland.

Bicycles gave girls and women much more freedom. Heavy skirts that stretched down to the ground started to give way to shorter lighter clothes. Soon women's ankles could be seen in public for the first time, breezing past on bicycles! And bicycles made it much easier for young women and men to spend time together. They could cycle off into the countryside away from nosy neighbours and without a chaperone always watching over them. Parents were alarmed, newspapers warned that nothing good would come of it; but for young Scots at the turn of the century the bicycle was a transport to new worlds.

Work to do . . .

1 The names Bouch, Fowler, Baker, and Arrol all have a place in the history of Scotland's railways. Who were they, and why did they become famous?

2 Where and when did the first motor cars appear? How soon afterwards was the first Scottish motor car built? Describe in your own words how Scotland's first car makers fared.

3 Read the extract from *The Wind in the Willows* again. Describe in your own words what Toad and the Rat think of motor cars. Whom do you agree with, and why?

Highlands and Islands

Crofters' Protest

During the nineteenth century, much of the Highlands was cleared of people to make way for sheep and deer. Some Highlanders headed for Glasgow and other lowland towns and cities. Others went abroad, to Canada, America, Australia or New Zealand. And those that stayed in the Highlands were crowded together in small areas of poor land near the coast.

As they tried to scrape a living out of their crofts, these Highlanders grew bitter and angry towards the landlords who owned the land. The landlords made their money out of sheep or from deer-stalking or grouse-shooting, not from crofters. Deer would eat the crofters' crops, and if the crofters kept dogs to protect their crops, the dogs would be shot by the landlord's gamekeeper. The crofters were not allowed to cut heather or rushes from the hills in case they disturbed the grouse, and so they could not repair the thatched roofs of their houses. They couldn't even complain to the local magistrate if the landlord broke the law, because the landlord often was the magistrate. Anger led to unrest. There were riots on Lewis in 1874. In 1882 things came to a head on Skye.

The Battle of Braes

Braes, the district of Skye running along the edge of the narrows of Raasay, was a typical crofting area. From May to September each year most of the young men left

their crofts to work with the fishing fleets as they followed the herring round the coast of Scotland. The women looked after the crofts: a few acres of land with a few sheep, perhaps a cow or a pig or a horse, and a potato patch.

For years the crofters' sheep had grazed on nearby Ben Lee. Then in 1882 the landlord suddenly denied them access. They tried to rent the land back from him, and when he refused they turned their sheep on to the hill anyway. The Sheriff of Inverness-shire ordered up a strong force of 60 policemen from Glasgow to evict the crofters, and at the crack of dawn one April morning this police force marched from Portree into Braes, arrested six men and set off back to Portree.

Outraged, hundreds of crofters from Braes and other settlements set off in pursuit. At one point they rained boulders from the top of a cliff onto the police on the road below. There were hand to hand fights, baton charges, split heads. Amazingly, no-one was killed, but when the police finally reached Portree with five prisoners there were many injuries to be attended to.

Feelings were running high among the crofters. More trouble flared up in Lewis, then in Glendale on Skye. Fences were pulled down, hay ricks were set ablaze. The newspapers had taken a big interest in the disturbances, and in the trial of the Braes men. The government began to panic, and sent warships and troops to Skye. But it was becoming obvious that the crofters could not be put down by force, that something had to be done to solve their problems. The press, the Church and public opinion in the Lowlands and in England always in the past had been hostile to the Highlanders. Now they started pushing for reforms, and in 1883 the government asked Lord Napier to lead an inquiry. His report revealed a shocking story. The Highlanders had faced, it said, 'a state of misery, of wrong-doing, and of patient long-suffering, without parallel in the history of our country.'

In 1885 the Highlanders put more pressure on the government when they elected four crofters MPs in a general election.

And so in 1886 the government passed the Crofters' Act, which is sometimes called the Magna Carta of the West Highlands. It put a stop to forced evictions and took away the landlord's right to charge whatever rent he liked. The crofters had gained a victory, the first for many a long year.

Angry crofters near Stornoway being read the Riot Act during disturbances in the 1880s. Reading the Riot Act gave the authorities the right to take stern measures to restore order.

Highland Homes

Above Inside a crofter's house at Loch Ewe, Wester Ross, in 1889
Right The faint outline of old lazybeds

A typical Highland home in the late nineteenth century was not a sooty tenement. It was a simple building called a 'black house', and could be found anywhere from the Outer Hebrides to Perthshire. It had very thick walls, four to eight feet thick. They were stone inside and out, and the hollow centre was filled up with earth or smaller stones. The walls were the same height all the way round. The roof was held up by beams across the top of the walls, covered in a thatch or just a thick mat of grass, heather, straw or rushes. The tops of the walls were often covered with turf, and sometimes sheep and lambs would graze up here.

Inside, the floor was often just flattened earth, with a fire in the middle and smoke everywhere. The furniture would be simple and often home-made: benches, stools, box beds and a table. Knives, forks and crockery were still uncommon, and so people often ate with their hands. At night, the home would be lit by candles made from sheep fat or fish liver, or by a simple dish of oil with a cloth rag for a wick. The door was never locked, and most doors had no key. In fact keys were a sign of meanness and lack of hospitality to the Highlander, and there was a saying in Gaelic 'cho mosach ris a ghlais' – 'as mean as the lock'.

Few crofts had a horse and cart. Sledges were used to move heavy loads, such as the peat cut for fuel, or the seaweed collected for fertilizer. And a horse would have been of little use to pull a plough over such small, stony and uneven patches of land. Instead a foot plough called the 'cas chrom' or bent foot plough was used. The soil was so thin and poor that crofters created an artificial raised plateau of soil called a rig, giving more depth of soil to grow crops like potatoes. These 'feannagan' or lazybeds can still be seen all over the Highlands as faint ridges near deserted houses.

Changes

The Glenfinnan Viaduct on the West Highland line between Fort William and Mallaig. When it was built in 1901, it was the first line in Britain to use concrete instead of stone or brick or steel in its bridges and viaducts. The builder, Robert McAlpine, was so keen on concrete that people nicknamed him 'Concrete Bob'.

Any observant late Victorian traveller would have noticed many changes taking place in the Highland way of life. Peat-cutting was giving way to coal, seaweed-collecting to artificial fertilizers. Corrugated iron was replacing thatch on the roofs. Again, the railways were bringers of change. In the 1870s they were pushed north from Helmsdale right up to Wick and Thurso in the far north. Then in 1894 the West Highland Railway was opened, running from Glasgow via Helensburgh through Crianlarich and then across the wilderness of Rannoch Moor to Spean Bridge and Fort William.

Fishing

With fast railway connections to the markets of the south, the fishing industry began to boom in northern Scotland. The idea of using steam-powered boats to drag a large bag-shaped net along the bottom of the sea had been developed in England. In the 1880s Aberdeen became the centre of this kind of fishing, known as trawling. Trawlers would set off on their long trips to the deep seas of the North Sea or Atlantic and return bulging with cod, haddock and other 'white fish'. In 1900 50,000 tonnes of fish were landed in Aberdeen, and by the outbreak of war in 1914 this had grown to over 115,000 tonnes, enough for at least a quarter of a *billion* fish suppers! As the harbour at Aberdeen became more crowded, new quays were built, then a new fishmarket. Torry by the harbour became the fastest-growing district of Aberdeen. Ice-factories, rope-works, net-repairers, fish-box makers and barrel-packers clustered round the harbour, and the air was filled with the smell of fish and the cries of seagulls.

From other Scottish ports, sailing boats went for the herring shoals as they migrated round the coasts of Britain. In spring these shoals were in the Minch, by May they had moved to the north, and by autumn were down the east coast as far as Great Yarmouth and Lowestoft. Stornoway on Lewis was a centre for the herring fishing, as was Castlebay on Barra, Scalpay on Harris, and Wick on the mainland. When the fishing fleet was in these ports, the sea seemed to vanish under hundreds of billowing brown sails. But after 1900, the sailing boats gave way to steamboats that could stay at sea following the herring, then land their catch at a railway port like Oban, Mallaig, or Fraserburgh.

The herring fleet crammed into Wick harbour, around 1895

Herring gutters at work in Wick. So many herring were brought ashore that thousands of women and girls followed the fleets around the coast, gutting the fish and packing them into barrels for export to Russia or Germany. From the North East ports alone, five or six hundred girls would go to the gutting from Fraserburgh, the same from Buckie, three hundred from Lossiemouth, two hundred from Hopeman. It was hard work. They worked at lightning speed, slicing open and gutting the fish, then packing them into barrels, carefully arranged row upon row, up to one thousand fish in a barrel. They wrapped their fingers carefully in strips of cloth to protect them from the flashing razor-sharp knives, but injuries happened. And for all that, a crew of three girls in 1911 would share 3 pence for each barrel. But although it was hard, it gave the girls some money of their own, a chance to live away from home with their friends, to buy clothes or treats. It gave them an independence they hadn't known before.

Harris Tweed

Other industries were also beginning to appear in the Highlands. On Harris, the islanders found that the tweeds they had made for generations could be sold to fashion houses in London and elsewhere. With the encouragement of the wife of the Earl of Dunmore, who owned the island, the making of tweed spread to South Uist, Barra and Lewis. At first, the work was done mainly by women at home. They picked berries and plants to make the dyes, they washed the wool, then 'carded' it to separate out the strands, then spun it into long strands, and finally wove it. The quality was superb, and no two 'webs' of tweed were the same. But by the end of the century machines to do these jobs were becoming more common, and some of the work moved out of the home into mills and factories. Men replaced women in this better-paid work. There was more quantity, but less quality.

The only problem with this new industry was that it was subject to fashion. Tweeds might be all the rage for a few years, then drop out of style. As fashion came and went, so did the fortunes of the Western Isles.

Below A woman weaving in Harris in 1910 on an old wooden loom
Inset The Orb Symbol.

The Harris tweed became so fashionable that soon material of the same name was being made in lowland Scotland, in Yorkshire, and in Japan. So in 1909 a Harris Tweed Association was set up to protect the industry. Only tweed made in the Outer Hebrides could be called 'Harris' tweed. Since the 1930s these tweeds have been marked with the Orb symbol.

Above Whisky advertisements, from around 1900 *Below* A distillery at Dalwhinnie

Another new Highland industry was whisky, the golden spirit that is sometimes called in Gaelic 'uisge bae' or 'the water of life'. The rest of the world knows it simply as Scotch. The only raw materials needed to make it are barley, peat and water, and the Highlands have plenty of all three.

The Highland whisky industry was given a big boost in the 1860s, when a disease hit the French grape harvest. Without grapes wine was scarce, without wine the wine spirit called brandy was scarce, and without brandy the English had no favourite tipple. Blended whisky stepped in. Walkers opened a London office in 1880, Dewars in 1884, and soon the English market was conquered. The Scots whisky makers then turned overseas. By 1886 Walkers were shipping their whisky to 45 different countries.

It was all good business for Scotland, bringing jobs and money into the country. But the Highlands saw little of it. The distilleries scattered through Speyside and up the west coast needed few people to run – thirty workers or less on average. Most of the work was in blending the whiskies, putting them in casks, storing them in huge bonded warehouses, and bottling and packaging them. And most of this work was done in the lowlands, in Leith, Edinburgh, Glasgow, Clydebank, or Kilmarnock.

Water Power for Aluminium

Highland water had other uses besides making whisky: it could be used to turn turbines that generated electricity. All that was needed was a reservoir or a dam across a river from which a constant supply of water could be drawn. Then the water would rush down pipes to a hall where the turbines lay waiting to be set spinning.

In the 1880s it was discovered that electricity could be used to smelt a new light metal called aluminium. The British Aluminium Company decided that the cheapest electricity could be had in the Highlands, and in 1896 opened a plant at the Falls of Foyers on the eastern shore of Loch Ness. It had its own hydro-electric supply, and was soon turning out two thousand tonnes a year of the new metal, about one-fifth of the world's production.

Aluminium became more and more popular. It could be used for anything from pots and pans to pistons, from earrings to engines. British Aluminium decided to open another much bigger factory, this time at Kinlochleven between Glencoe and Fort William. Work began in 1903 and went on for four years. High above Kinlochleven in the mountains a huge dam was built at Blackwater. When it was finished, the wall holding back the water was over 900 metres long.

Thousands of navvies were attracted to the Kinlochleven construction site, for these big projects still depended on muscle power and lots of it. One of them was called Patrick McGill, and later he wrote a book about it called *Children of the Dead End*. It tells the story of how he was born into a poor family of thirteen in Donegal, Ireland, left school at ten, and came to Scotland with a gang of potato pickers when he was 14. He worked on the railways around Glasgow for a while, then drifted north to Kinlochleven. There he meets scenes like the Wild West, full of danger and daring, gambling and fighting, with men called Moleskin Joe, Carroty Dan or Two-Shift Mullholland. He works through biting cold and baking heat, digging, blasting, hammering, shovelling. And he thinks more and more about his surroundings and his life as a navvy:

'All around the ancient mountains sat like brooding witches, dreaming on their own story of which they knew neither the beginning nor the end. Naked to the four winds of heaven and all the rains of the world, they had stood there for countless ages in all their sinister strength, undefied and unconquered, until man, with puny hands and little tools of labour, came to break the spirit of their ancient mightiness.

And we, the men who braved this task, were outcasts of the world . . . We were men flogged to the work which we had to do, and hounded from the work which we had accomplished. We were men despised when we were most useful, rejected when we were not needed, and forgotten when our troubles weighed upon us heavily.

Even as I thought of these things a shoulder of jagged rock fell into a cutting far below. There was the sound of a scream in the distance, and a song died away in the throat of some rude singer. Then out of the pit I saw men, red with the muck of the deep earth and redder still with the blood of a stricken mate, come forth, bearing between them a silent figure. Another of the pioneers of civilisation had given up his life for the sake of society.'

On Hogmanay 1907 Kinlochleven produced its first aluminium, and within a few years one third of the world's aluminium was coming from Scotland.

Workmen building the aluminium works at Foyers, Inverness-shire, in 1896. It was the first modern factory in the Highlands.

The Highland Playground

Each estate owner wanted a lodge that was grander than his neighbour's lodge. Fantastic mansions sprang up in the wilds, with towers and battlements and turrets. The picture shows the main hall at Kinloch Castle on the island of Rhum. Stalkers and their assistants or 'ghillies' were employed to guide wealthy guests from the lodge to the deer and back.

By the end of the nineteenth century the old suspicions and fears of the Highlands had disappeared. Sir Walter Scott had made them romantic. Queen Victoria with her highland home at Balmoral had made them fashionable, and the railways had made them easy for southerners to get to.

The pastime that brought the biggest changes was the shooting of deer for sport. Brewers, distillers, shipowners and steelmasters became interested in this sport and started to buy Highland estates. Soon more money could be made from deerstalking than from sheep farming. So the land that had been cleared of people to make way for sheep, was now cleared of sheep to make way for deer. By 1900 no less than one and a quarter million hectares of Scotland was turned over to the deer.

Stalking had critics: people who thought it was wasteful or cruel. But the sport created jobs, and the total number of deer grew and grew. By 1912 there were around 180,000 deer on the Highland estates, more than the number of people in the whole Western Highlands.

Other sports were less exclusive. The mountains were slowly being explored by walkers and climbers. Clubs began to form, like the Cobbler Club of Glasgow, which started in 1866 and was named after the Cobbler mountain above Arrochar. In 1889 the new sport came of age when the Scottish Mountaineering Club was formed in Glasgow. Just two years later one of its members, Sir Hugh Munro, made a list of all the mountains in Scotland over 3000 feet high. By his reckoning there were 538, a target for future climbers.

Left A Scottish Mountaineering Club meet at Dundonnell in 1910. Sir Hugh Munro is in the middle. *Right* A modern Mod in Oban

Following its rapidly growing popularity in the Alps, ski-ing, too, started to appear in the Highlands at the turn of the century. W. W. Naismith, a founder member of the Scottish Mountaineering Club, was practising on the Campsies just north of Glasgow in 1890. By 1907 a Scottish Ski Club had been formed, and was soon exploring Ben Nevis, Drumochter and Tyndrum.

Others came to the Highlands for less energetic pastimes. Towns like Strathpeffer and Ballater began to develop as health resorts or 'spas' famous for their mineral waters. Visitors could stay in comfortable hotels amidst beautiful surroundings, taking the waters and feeling that they were improving their health.

And so, with all this new activity in the Highlands, there was at last some reason to be optimistic about the future. In 1891 the Highlanders took a step to protect their place in that future. They formed An Comunn Gaidhealach, a Highland Society to encourage Gaelic language, song, dance, music and arts. They held their first annual gathering in Oban in 1892. Called the Mod, it started at 11 in the morning, and for four hours 40 competitors performed their skills and tried to win the 12 prizes that were being awarded. It was not an instant success, in fact a man had to be posted at the door to try to get the good folk of Oban to come in and see what was happening. But it was a start.

Work to do . . .

1 Pretend you are a journalist who has been sent to Skye in 1886. Now write a report for your newspaper about the new Crofters' Act, and the events that led up to it. If you want to, make up some interviews with local people, or eyewitness accounts, and include them in your report.

2 The old Highland 'black house' was very different from a modern home. What was different about the walls; the roof; the floor; the lighting; the fire; the furniture?

3 Here are two lists, one of places and the other of industries. **Places**: Kinlochleven, Strathpeffer, Castlebay, Kilmarnock, Ballater, Harris, Wick, Falls of Foyers, Mallaig.
Industries: fishing, whisky, tweed, tourism, aluminium.
Now match the places with the industries.

Departures and Arrivals

Departures

Left Advert in the Govan Press, 1906 *Above* Gaelic, French and English at a post office in Iona, Canada

Before 1880, most of the people who left Scotland to start a new life elsewhere were quite poor. Many were Highlanders who had been evicted, or handloom weavers made unemployed by new technology. After 1880, a far wider range of people left. Many had skills, as miners, bakers, joiners or farmers. Others were clerks or teachers, people with qualifications. Nowadays we would describe the emigration of people like this as a 'brain drain.'

Between 1881 and 1890 over 217,000 people left Scotland. The numbers fell in the years from 1891 to 1900, and then soared again at the beginning of the twentieth century. In the ten years from 1901 to 1910 over 254,000 people left Scotland for a life elsewhere. That comes to 500 people every week, for ten years.

Famous Scots Abroad

Canada was where the Scots had not only settled in large numbers, but had set up a new Scotland: Nova Scotia. It was Donald Smith from Morayshire and his cousin George Stephen who were behind the building of the Canadian Pacific Railway. Two other Scots, Donald Mann and William McKenzie, pushed through the rival Canadian Northern Railway. Canada's first 2

Prime Ministers were Scottish, John MacDonald and Alexander MacKenzie, a stone-mason from Dunkeld.

Australia and New Zealand also have many links with Scotland. Robert Stout, a schoolteacher from Orkney, emigrated to New Zealand and became Prime Minister in 1884. Andrew Fisher, an Ayrshire miner, became Australia's Prime Minister in 1908, the first Labour Prime Minister in the world. In fact, by the turn of the century there had been a dozen Scots-born Prime Ministers in Australia and New Zealand.

Carnegie

It was in America that many Scottish emigrants found the best opportunities. One of America's largest companies, Bell Telephone, still carries the name of Alexander Graham Bell, born in Edinburgh in 1847, the Scottish emigrant who invented the telephone. But the most famous emigrant of all was Andrew Carnegie. He was born in Dumfermline in Fife in 1835. His father was a weaver, a trade that was being killed off by new machines and new ways of working. His mother was the one who had to worry about bringing up Andrew, and making ends meet.

Mother and father had different views of the world. Carnegie's father was a radical. He supported political action, and favoured a charter of rights for working men: he was a 'Chartist'. He had been arrested once by the government for sedition. Carnegie's mother took a dim view of all this: it didn't, she said, 'put the food on the table or the silver in the sporran'. To her, life was a hard fight for survival in which you had to be selfish and think of yourself first. She persuaded Carnegie's father to make a fresh start, and in 1848 the family emigrated to Allegheny near Pittsburgh in Pennsylvania.

Andrew Carnegie took a job in the new industry of telegraphy, and by the age of 18 had become telegraphist and secretary to a railroad baron called Scott. Scott was impressed with his 'white-haired Scotch

An elderly Andrew Carnegie (centre) leaving a meeting in New York

devil', and started giving him business tips. Soon Carnegie was buying and selling, dealing and speculating. By 1868 he had the income of a millionaire. At this stage he had doubts about his future. Perhaps he was torn between the examples of his mother and his father. But Carnegie's doubts did not last. Soon he was scrabbling towards greater wealth. Steel became his life, his great factories at Pittsburgh pouring out thousands of tonnes every week. Nothing and no-one were allowed to stand in his way. In 1892 workers on strike at his Homestead factory were brutally beaten into submission by a private police force. When Carnegie finally sold his company in 1900, he received over 300 million dollars.

Carnegie had the 'worm of immortality' in him. He wanted to be remembered, not for the Homestead strike, but for doing good. He felt that 'he who dies rich dies disgraced.' So for the remaining 19 years of his life he set about spending his money. Libraries were given to hundreds of towns and cities in Scotland and many other countries. By 1910 half the university students in Scotland were getting help to pay their fees from a Carnegie Fund for Universities. He spent much of his time at Skibo Castle, near Dornoch in Sutherland. When he died, in 1919, he had managed to spend his fortune.

Missionaries

Not every Scottish emigrant went forth seeking fame and fortune. In India, the West Indies, China and especially Africa, hundreds of Scots were at work as Christian missionaries. Their mission was to teach Christianity, but this was done in many different ways. Some were medical missionaries, bringing new ideas and methods of scientific medicine to other countries. Some were trading missionaries, wishing to set up companies, colonies, farms. Some were educational missionaries, establishing schools in remote villages. Sometimes these activities became more important than teaching Christianity. Desmond Tutu, the South African bishop and Nobel Prize winner, once remarked

that 'when the white man came here, we had the land and he had God. He said close your eyes and pray to God. We did, and when we opened our eyes we had God and he had the land.'

Mary Slessor became one of the best-known Scottish missionaries to follow David Livingstone of Blantyre to Africa. She was born in 1848 in Aberdeen, and moved to Dundee with her family when she was ten. There she worked long hours in the jute mills, six hours a day at a loom, another six hours at the mill school. She read reports of foreign missions in her church magazine, and in 1875 she boarded the African Steamship line's *S.S. Ethiopia* for the long voyage to Calabar in Nigeria on the west coast of Africa. There she began her work as a missionary for the United Presbyterian Church.

The missionary work of Mary Slessor and others like her often improved the lives of people in Africa and elsewhere. But there could also be bad effects. It was too easy to think that Europeans were somehow superior to others, and had a right to interfere all over the world, even to take over things. At the same time as white Europeans like Mary Slessor were fighting against cruelty, other white Europeans were spreading it. There was a 'scramble for Africa', as European countries rushed to grab land in Africa by force. Belgium, Portugal, Germany, France, Italy were all involved. But Britain was more involved than anyone. And Scottish traders, soldiers, and settlers were to the fore in the British scramble.

Mary Slessor tried to stop the trade in alcohol that the Europeans found so profitable. She tried to encourage commerce, and her efforts came to be respected by the people of Calabar. They started to call her Our Ma: 'Our Ma is Eka Kpukpru owo, the mother of all people', they said. When she died in 1915, she was buried in Calabar. The photograph below shows Mary Slessor at her West African mission station. She is surrounded by some of the people with whom she spent most of her life.

Arrivals

This Jewish cap-making factory was photographed in 1905. It was in Oxford Street in Glasgow's Gorbals. Oxford Street was at the centre of Glasgow's Jewish community; in it was a synagogue and a 'Zionist Free Reading Room and Library', alongside stores and workshops run by Scottish Jews.

The migration of people was not all in the same direction. Many people left Scotland, but some also came to Scotland from other countries.

In the 1890s people from Lithuania started arriving in numbers in Scotland. Lithuania was a largely agricultural country in Eastern Europe. Conditions there were very bad, and between 1870 and 1914 650,000 people left. That was almost a quarter of the population. Most went to America, but by 1914 around 6,000 had settled in the coal, iron and steel areas of Lanarkshire, particularly around Coatbridge. Some were recruited by Lanarkshire coalmine owners to come to Scotland and break strikes. Others were en route to America and decided to stay. And once some had made a home in Lanarkshire, they arranged for friends and relatives to come and join them. By the early years of the century streets in Carfin, New Stevenson and Bellshill had become Lithuanian, with rows of name-plates such as *Yafortskus, Baukauskus, Kredera* and *Koshinsky*. Sometimes the mine manager or gaffer, having difficulty with the Lithuanian surname of a worker, would change it, and odd names were invented: Frank Gorilla, Joseph Coalbag, Antanas Kipper. By 1914 the Lithuanians in Lanarkshire had recreated a community life, with their own shops, churches, societies, and newspapers.

Jews, too, started arriving in Scotland between the 1880s and 1914. Mostly they came from Poland and Russia, and were trying to escape poverty and persecution.

One woman, called Mrs Brauerman, remembers her childhood:

'I come frae Dubna guberniya in Russia and I was born, I think, in 1891. I remember I was always running around, going to the market. It was in a big square and the old ladies used to sit with the shawls round them, freezing cold . . . Everybody was poor. The pogroms were gettin' so bad that I was told they used to go into a house and they'd pull a baby's tongue out! I was told that and I felt terrible . . . people were nervous in case things got worse and that's the reason they left because things weren't so good.'

Glasgow was the main destination in Scotland, for there had long been a small Jewish community in Glasgow, and a new synagogue had been built in Garnethill in 1879. The new arrivals tended to settle in the Gorbals on the south side of the river. There they started many small businesses: as furniture makers, tailors, shoe makers and repairers, travellers, and pawnbrokers. By 1903 about 6,000 Jews had moved to Scotland, and two-thirds of them lived in the Gorbals.

These new Scots were tolerated, but they were not openly accepted. Established Protestant and Catholic churches were sometimes hostile to the Jews, and many landlords refused to let houses to Jews. Housing in the Gorbals was a big improvement on the ghettoes of Eastern Europe, but it was still bad. When the Jews started moving out of the Gorbals into better housing, it was largely through their own efforts.

At first many of Scotland's Italian arrivals sold ice-cream from barrows. They might push their barrows miles to make a few pennies. 'Ecce un poco, senore' they would cry, which literally means 'here is a little, Sir.' This was misunderstood by local people as 'Hokey Pokey' and soon the ice-cream sellers became known as Hokey Pokey men. This photo shows one of them at the turn of the century.

A third group of immigrants to Scotland before the First World War came from Italy. About 4,000 Italians came to Scotland between 1890 and 1914. Most came from very poor farming areas, in particular from the district of Lucca in Northern Italy, and from Frasinore in the Abruzzi, south of Rome. They came with little or nothing, and by the cheapest way possible. When they arrived in Glasgow or Edinburgh, the most common form of work for Italians was making and selling ice-cream.

By 1914 most towns and villages in Scotland could sport at least one ice-cream parlour, or a fish and chip shop, run by Italians.

Dominic Crolla's family and friends all came to Scotland from Italy:

'I had a friend in Edinburgh whose father, when he died, we were all up in his house and we were looking for his birth certificate. When we came across it in a drawer we discovered that his father in 1904 or 1905 had been born on the roadside between Dover and London. You see these people had walked from Italy, they'd got lifts on horses and carts and they made their way from the middle of Italy by road and track and boat to London.'

Work to do . . .

1 Find out whether you have any relatives in other countries. If you have, try to discover when they or their ancestors emigrated from Scotland. When everyone in the class has done the same, add up the results to see which country has most relatives, and the years in which emigration from Scotland was highest.
2 Describe in your own words the lives of Andrew Carnegie and Mary Slessor. In your opinion, what are the main similarities and differences between them?
3 Who were some of the main groups of immigrants to Scotland between 1880 and 1914? Why had they left their native country? Where in Scotland did they tend to settle?

Kailyard and Canvas

Robert Louis Stevenson

A portrait of Robert Louis Stevenson, painted in 1887

Kidnapped: 'I was cast upon a little barren isle.' The painting is by N. C. Wye

Towards the end of the nineteenth century a wave of activity swept across Scottish writing, painting, and architecture. And out of it all emerged a few Scots good enough to become famous around the world.

One of them was Robert Louis Stevenson. He was born in Edinburgh in 1850. His father and grandfather were both well-known engineers who specialised in building lighthouses. In fact some of Britain's most famous lighthouses are Stevenson lights, and they also built a chain of them right round the coast of Japan.

Young Robert went to university to study engineering. He was all set to continue the family tradition. But then he changed his mind. He dropped engineering and became a lawyer. He began to travel, and to write about his journeys.

He described a canoe trip in Belgium, a donkey ride in France, a voyage across the Atlantic, a railway journey across America. His skill as a writer grew. Then in 1881 he spent a summer holiday in Braemar. While it rained, he invented a story to entertain the young people in the house. It was an adventure story, about hidden treasure, pirates and South Sea islands. It was a gripping tale, fast moving and well-told. It was full of colourful characters, like the pirate Long John Silver with a peg-leg. Stevenson called the story *Treasure Island*, and published it in 1883. It was a big success, and has become one of the classic adventure stories of all time.

Other adventures followed. In 1886 Stevenson published *Kidnapped*. It throws together lowlander David Balfour and Highlander Alan Breck Stewart, and follows them across the Highlands just after the 1745 rebellion. Like *Treasure Island*, *Kidnapped* has remained popular ever since it first appeared.

But Stevenson was not just a writer of adventures. In 1886 he published a book called *The Strange Case of Dr Jekyll and Mr Hyde*. It is a frightening tale of a man with a split personality, part good and part evil. The struggle between these two parts of him lead to his death, but not before he has killed others.

Some people have argued that the Jekyll & Hyde story is a very Scottish story, and that the Scottish character is divided. For example, they point out that the Scots are Scottish and British at the same time, that they are dour but also romantic, realistic but also reckless, scientific yet sentimental, Highland and Lowland. Whatever the truth of this, it is certainly true that Stevenson had divided feelings about Scotland. Books like *Kidnapped* are filled with loving descriptions of the mountains and moors, yet he felt he had to move abroad to escape the dullness and climate of Edinburgh. Eventually he settled in 1889 on the island of Samoa in the South Seas, and he died and was buried there in 1894.

The Kailyard

A scene from a modern production of J. M. Barrie's play *Peter Pan*: 'Every time a child says "I don't believe in fairies" there is a little fairy somewhere that falls down dead'.

Robert Louis Stevenson was the best Scottish writer of his time, but the writers who sold most books were a small group that was nicknamed the 'Kailyard' or cabbage-patch school. Chief amongst them was James M. Barrie, who was born in Kirriemuir in Angus in 1860.

Barrie went to Edinburgh University and later moved to London as a journalist. It was there that he started writing stories about life in Kirriemuir, which he called *Thrums*. These stories were very popular, and soon other writers were writing the same sort of stuff. John Watson, an English minister, changed his name to Ian Maclaren and wrote a series of stories about a village that he called *Drumtochty*. It was based on the Perthshire village of Logiealmond, where he worked as a minister. Then there was Samuel R. Crockett, who was born in Balmaghie, Kirkcudbrightshire, in 1859. He too trained as a minister but was so successful as a writer that he devoted all his time to it. He published more than 40 novels, mostly written at his home in Peebles.

Books by Barrie, Maclaren and Crockett sold by the million. They were especially popular in England and the United States. The world they described in their stories was make-believe, with nothing at all about cities, factories, science or slums. Instead they were about rural life, about villages and village worthies, solid teachers, shrewd housekeepers, honest farmers and greedy landlords. They were sentimental and romantic, and looked backwards through rose-tinted spectacles to a past that had never existed. Probably, that was why they were so popular, for many people preferred to read about a make-believe past than a brutally real present.

Even so, the popularity of the Kailyard writers made some people angry. George Douglas Brown, for instance, knew that village life was not like *Thrums* or *Drumtochty*, or that, if it was, it was nothing to be pleased about. In 1901 he published a book called *The House with the Green Shutters*. He called his village Barbie, based on the Ayrshire village of Ochiltree near where he had been born in 1869. But his village is not described in a sentimental way. 'Only ten decent folk in the book, and about thirty brutes, ruffians and fools', he said. Barbie is full of sour gossiping and sly sneering, of hypocrites and liars. It is a dreadful place full of dreadful people.

The Kailyard stories also upset a novelist from Tarbert on Loch Fyne called John Macdougall Hay. In 1914 he published a book called *Gillespie*, based on a west coast fishing village that he calls Brierton. It is a story about a ruthless man called Gillespie Strang. This man is full of ambition and greed, and lets nothing stand in his way. As he takes over control of more and more lives in the village, his wife is pushed towards alcoholic destruction. Eventually his sons turn against him and bring about his downfall.

Gillespie and *The House with the Green Shutters* both set out to attack the Kailyard view of Scotland. And both are powerful, well-written novels that are still read today. But despite their attacks, the Kailyard continued to be popular. In time it would start appearing not just in books, but in newspapers, radio programmes and TV serials.

And finally, J. M. Barrie again. He didn't just write about *Thrums*. In 1904 he wrote a play called *Peter Pan*. It is about a boy who won't grow up, and is full of pirates, redskins, fairies, and mermaids, of the 'never never land', the 'lost boys' and the 'home under the ground'. It was an instant success in 1904, and has been hugely popular ever since. When Barrie died in 1937, Peter Pan had already joined the immortals.

George Washington Wilson

In 1839 the invention of photography was announced to the world. Within a few years photographers were at work in many countries. A few were very successful, and built a thriving business.

One Scotsman who did so was George Washington Wilson. He had been born in a croft a few miles south of Banff in 1823. In Edinburgh he trained as an artist, but became more and more interested in photography. And when he opened a studio in Aberdeen in 1849 he soon became aware that photography would threaten his portrait business unless he moved into it. Soon he was offering paintings or photographs, and his business was growing.

Wilson had a lucky break in 1854. Queen Victoria and Prince Albert had decided to rebuild Balmoral Castle on Deeside and asked Wilson to take photographs of the building work. They were pleased with the results, and soon Wilson the 'Royal Photographer' was a regular visitor to Balmoral, clambering over the hills and through the forests of Deeside to take landscape photographs with his bulky equipment.

These landscape photographs were the making of Wilson. More and more tourists wanted to buy photographs of places they had visited. Wilson made sure he had one to sell. Fingal's Cave, Westminster Abbey, Stonehenge, Glencoe, Killiecrankie, Iona, Abbotsford were all photographed. His photographs, with the famous G.W.W. initials on them, could be bought all over Britain, in railway bookstalls, hotels, shops, and ships. By the 1860s he was so successful that his photograph printing works on the outskirts of Aberdeen was producing over half a million prints each year.

And still the company grew. By the 1890s it was offering photographs taken all over the British Isles, and in Gibraltar, Spain, Morocco, South Africa and Australia. But Wilson was becoming a sick man, suffering frequent fits. Perhaps they had been caused by his many years of work with photographic chemicals. Perhaps the hardships of his photographic tours to wild and inaccessible places had exhausted him. In 1893 he died. His business slowly wound down, and in 1908 the whole lot was sold in an auction. G.W.W. had dominated the world of photographic landscapes, but his work had gone out of style, replaced by the new postcard industry. 65,000 negatives were sold off for just a couple of hundred pounds. Many of the photographs he had taken personally were left unsold. G.W.W.'s work could easily have been lost forever, but fortunately most of the photographs survived, and are now stored safely in the library of Aberdeen University. Once again we can look at Scotland the way he saw it a hundred years ago.

Scottish Painters

The invention of photography made many nineteenth century painters change the way they painted, and try to see the world around them in a way that no photograph could ever capture. One was William MacTaggart, who was born in 1835 and died in 1910. He was attracted to the west coast of Scotland, with its surf and winds and wide skies. He worked outdoors almost all the time, and not in a studio. One photograph taken in 1898 shows him standing on the shore at Macrihanish, in front of a canvas so large that it had to be tied down by ropes attached to boulders to stop it blowing away!

As MacTaggart painted, he concentrated on capturing his *impressions* of what he saw. The titles of his paintings show clearly what interested him most: *Through Wind and Rain*; *Something out of the Sea*; *Away to the West as the Sun Went Down*; *The Wave*; *The Storm*.

MacTaggart didn't bother very much about what other painters were doing. But in fact his approach to painting was shared by other painters. In France a small group of painters such as Claude Monet and August Renoir had also decided to paint their impressions of what they saw. They too concentrated on light, reflections, shimmers, hazes, colours, clouds and shadows. At the time, most people made fun of them or ignored them or thought they were mad. Nowadays their paintings are sold for millions of pounds. They are now known as Impressionists, and it seems right that MacTaggart should be known as the Scottish Impressionist.

G. W. W.'s photographic works at St. Swithin's, Aberdeen. Glass negatives and paper were placed in daylight to make prints.

The Coming of St Columba by William MacTaggart. This famous painting is in the National Gallery of Scotland, Edinburgh.

William MacTaggart was a bit of a loner, working away by himself and for himself. But other painters tended to work together in 'schools' or 'groups', and the most famous in Scotland was the group of Glasgow painters called the 'Glasgow Boys'. They thought a lot of the work done by other Scottish painters was too sugary and sentimental, and that it was more concerned with making money than with being good. And they thought that artists in other countries, like the Impressionists, were doing more interesting things than artists in Scotland. So they wanted to import new ideas.

The Glasgow Boys didn't last for long as a group: their best years were from about 1885 to 1895. But they caused some big changes in Scottish painting. They made it less sentimental and a bit more realistic. And they made the public a bit more interested in looking at paintings and buying paintings. Some of the Glasgow Boys' names to look out for in art galleries are W. Y. MacGregor, James Guthrie, John Lavery, George Henry and E. A. Walton.

A Galloway Landscape by George Henry

William Burrell

Sir William Burrell

The Glasgow Boys, and other Scottish painters, had a new source of help and encouragement by the end of the nineteenth century. Scotland's industrial wealth had produced a number of wealthy businessmen who were interested in using their money to build art collections. One of them was William Allen Coats, a member of the Paisley thread family. Another was Arthur Kay, a partner in a large warehouse firm in Glasgow. But the most famous was William Burrell.

Burrell was born in Glasgow in 1861. His family owned a shipping company, and he started work as a clerk in the office when he was 14. He seems to have been very good with figures and money, while his brother George knew all about the technical side of ships. So when their father died in 1885 the two brothers took over the firm, and seem to have formed an ideal partnership.

Shipping is a business that tends to go through 'booms' and 'slumps'. For a while business is good, with plenty of contracts to carry cargo and good profits to be made. So shipowners build more ships, and business is also good in the shipyards. This is the 'boom'. But it can't last: once new ships are built there is more competition for cargo, and new ships aren't needed. So profits fall, shipbuilding stops, and a 'slump' has arrived.

Before the First World War these booms and slumps affected Glasgow's shipping very badly. They happened every six or seven years. But the Burrell brothers found a way to benefit. They waited until the height of a boom, when every shipowner was desperate for more ships at any price, and then sold all their ships to the highest bidder. Then they just sat on the cash and waited a few years for the slump to arrive. When it did,

and shipbuilders were desperate for work to keep their yards going, the Burrell brothers would arrange to have a brand-new fleet built at rock-bottom prices. Come the next boom they sold them off at huge profits and started all over again.

It was a game that required nerves of steel, but it made the Burrells extremely wealthy. William could afford to start collecting works of art. We will return to his collection later in the book.

Charles Rennie Mackintosh

Scotland at the turn of the century was an interesting place to be an architect. All around the country architects were getting orders to design new structures: offices, warehouses, factories, stations, hotels, docks, schools, houses, bridges, churches and shops. It was in this environment that Scotland produced its most important architect for a century: Charles Rennie Mackintosh.

He was born in Glasgow in 1868. His father was a police superintendent and the family was a typical size for the time. Charles was the second son of a family of eleven boys and girls. He left school when he was 16 and started training to be an architect: during the day he worked as an apprentice, in the evenings he went to classes at Glasgow School of Art. At the school he found there was a buzz of excitement. The Glasgow Boys were beginning to make themselves known, and the school had a new head, an Englishman called Fra Newbery. By the 1890's Newbery had turned the school into one of the finest art schools in Britain. So Mackintosh was surrounded by people from whom he could get ideas and inspiration.

When he finished training and started work it soon became obvious that he had a rare talent. His senior partners in the business gave him more and more opportunity to design buildings they were working on.

Charles Rennie Mackintosh

What is so special about Mackintosh's Art School? (shown right) This is the cause of many arguments, and there is no simple answer. One thing is that it is a very good building to work in. The studios are well designed to let in daylight, the library is cleverly designed to provide room for studying. In other words, it is a very *functional* building. But it is also rather splendid and dramatic to look at, and pleases the eye. From the outside the two ends look a bit like an old Scottish baronial castle, while the front is decorated with wonderful wrought-iron railings and brackets.

Then in 1896 came his big break. The Glasgow School of Art wanted to build new premises in Gilmorehill off Sauchiehall Street. Mackintosh's firm won the competition to design it, and the job was given to Mackintosh. The result was a building admired by architects all over Europe.

Apart from the School of Art, Mackintosh designed some other famous buildings. Near Kilmacolm in Renfrewshire he designed a private house called Windyhill, and near Helensburgh he built a home called Hill House for the publisher Walter Blackie. And in Glasgow he designed some famous tea-rooms for a woman called Miss Cranston. The best-known were the Willow Tea-rooms in Sauchiehall Street.

He was admired all over Europe, but in his home country Mackintosh did not get much support. Hardly any new orders for buildings were given to him after the Art School was finished in 1909. In Glasgow people poked fun at the tearooms, with their 'gae fancy' doors and 'arty' windows. In 1913 Mackintosh resigned from his work in Glasgow, and left the country. His wife was a gifted painter, and tried to encourage him to continue working, but he had lost heart, and took to drink. Then in 1923 Margaret persuaded him that they should move to a little village called Port Vendres on the Mediterranean coast of France. There he too began painting, and produced some beautiful water-colour paintings of flowers and of landscapes. But this new life was to be a short one, for he became ill, and died in 1928. When the contents of his studios were sold off, the valuers described them as being of 'practically no value'. Only long after his death did his home country see that he was a genius, and begin to look after and cherish the heritage he had left.

The Willow Tea-rooms, Sauchiehall Street, Glasgow. Mackintosh liked to design everything in his buildings, from the walls and windows right down to the furniture, lights, cutlery and curtains. He paid great attention to detail, and made sure that the builders working for him did exactly as he said. Sometimes his perfectionism drove them to despair: as one of his joiners said, 'there was nae palaver wi' Charlie.'

Work to do . . .

1 a Who wrote: *Peter Pan*; *Kidnapped*; *The House with the Green Shutters?*
b Compare in your own words a village like 'Thrums' or 'Drumtochty' with a village like 'Barbie'.
2 Study the painting by William MacTaggart, and write a description of it to someone who has not seen it. Write a paragraph saying whether or not you like it, and why.

3 What line of business did the Burrell family follow? Describe in your own words how William Burrell built his fortune.
4 Look at the photograph of the Glasgow School of Art, then list the differences between it and a modern school or office.

Politics and Power

One Man, One Vote!

At the beginning of Scotland's Industrial Revolution, the business of running the country lay in the hands of a very small number of men. Most of them came from the old aristocratic families that owned the land.

It wasn't a democratic system. In fact hardly anyone had a vote to decide who went to Parliament. Before 1832 only 5000 Scots had a vote, although the population was over two million.

But ideas about fairness and good government were changing. Aristocratic rule was no longer acceptable to many people. Already there had been revolutions in America and France against the old system.

Another force for change was the Industrial Revolution itself. As Scotland's towns and cities swelled, and as new industries arose, so the pattern of wealth and power changed. Land was no longer the only source of power – so were the banks and mines and steelworks and shipyards. More and more people began to demand a say in things.

First, it was the turn of men in the newly important middle class jobs: the traders, lawyers, bankers and businessmen. They were too powerful to ignore and in 1832 a Reform Act was passed by Parliament giving them the vote. The number of voters in Scotland jumped to 65,000.

Next it was the turn of the masons, bakers, carpenters, weavers and other skilled workmen. In 1868 a Second Reform Act gave them the vote, and so 230,000 men in Scotland could take part in elections.

Still the pressure continued. 'One man one vote' was a cry for universal male suffrage. In Scotland this meant great support for the Liberal leader William Gladstone, who was seen as more in favour of another voting reform than his opponent, the Tory leader Benjamin Disraeli. In fact the Scottish support for Gladstone was so great that in 1879 he decided to stand for election as Member of Parliament for Midlothian.

His campaign caused a sensation. It was the very first 'whistle-stop' election campaign. Gladstone travelled around in a special train, which was covered in flags, thistles and bunting and had a bust of him on the front of the engine. He could travel from one packed hall to another, and if there was no hall for him to speak in, he would just lean out of the train window and speak from there! No-one could compete with him, and he won the seat easily.

The tide of protest was so strong that in 1884 a Third Reform Act was passed. It more than doubled the number of electors in Scotland. Now farmworkers, crofters, miners, and other working-class men could vote and have a say in deciding who should represent them in Parliament.

By 1884 the only thing in the way of another Reform Act was the House of Lords. It was filled with people who had inherited their power and didn't want to give it up. Their resistance caused huge demonstrations. One of the biggest was in Glasgow, where 64,000 people marched through the streets to Glasgow Green, to be met by another 200,000 people who had gathered to cheer them. The marchers held aloft hundreds of portraits of Gladstone, and giant banners with messages to the Lords. 'The crooked Lords – we'll cut them straight' said the sawyard workers' banner, while the furniture polishers' banner threatened to 'polish off the Lords'. This drawing of Glasgow's Great Franchise Demonstration appeared in a magazine called *The Bailie* in 1884.

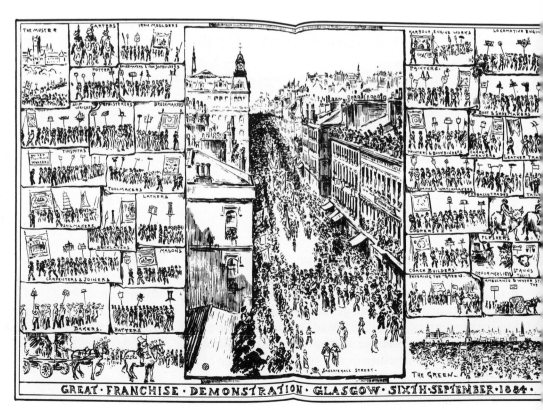

GREAT · FRANCHISE · DEMONSTRATION · GLASGOW · SIXTH · SEPTEMBER · 1884 ·

Gladstone on his 'whistle-stop' campaign in 1870: a modern impression

The timeline chart within the image shows:

1800	5,000 Scots Men have a vote
1825	
	← 1832 Reform Act
	65,000 Scots Men have a vote
1850	
	← 1868 Second Reform Act
1875	230,000 Scots Men have a vote
	← 1884 Third Reform Act
	500,000 Scots Men have a vote
1900	

Votes for Women

The 1884 reform was a step forward, but it still left Britain a long way short of being a full democracy. Four out of every ten men still were denied a vote. And women were left out completely.

Women had fewer rights than men in other areas too. For instance, there were lots of jobs they weren't allowed to do, like being a lawyer or a doctor. One woman, an English woman called Sophia Jex Blake, had become famous in 1869 by her campaign to study medicine at Edinburgh University. She did become Scotland's first woman doctor in 1877, but only by going to Berne in Switzerland to study and get a qualification.

But it was becoming more and more difficult to continue treating women so unequally. Alone, at home, looking after house and family, they were easy to ignore. But more and more women were going out to work. The typewriter, invented in 1867, had created a huge number of new office jobs that were almost all done by women. And the telephone had been another invention that created tens of thousands of jobs for women at the switchboards. And apart from these new industries, there were the mills and factories. In Dundee a woman was as likely to be the main wage-earner in a family as a man.

Paid jobs made women more difficult to ignore or treat badly. In the 1870s and 1880s women held many strikes for more pay and better conditions: in 1871 at the Wallace Factory, Perth and the Broadford Mill in Aberdeen; in 1873 at the Nithsdale Mill; in 1875 at the Baltic jute mills, Glasgow. And some improvements were made. In 1889, for example, Parliament passed an Act that made it possible for women to go to university in Scotland.

Women at work: Glasgow Central Old Telephone Exchange around 1890

A National Suffrage Demonstration in Princes Street, Edinburgh, 1909

But one thing that no government seemed ready to do was give women the vote. And the longer they delayed, the more impatient some women became. Amongst them were Mrs Christabel Pankhurst and her daughter Sylvia Pankhurst. They launched their campaign in 1902 in England, calling it the Women's Social and Political Union. It started in Manchester, and for a few years it didn't make much impact. Then in 1906, at a Liberal meeting in Manchester, Christabel stood up to ask what the Liberal policy was on votes for women. She was dragged out of the hall by stewards. Outside, she was arrested for causing an obstruction and spitting at a policeman. She was sent to prison for 7 days, and the publicity was enormous. Every newspaper in the country ran stories, and the *Daily Mail* provided a name for the protesting women – suffragettes. From then on, the Pankhursts relied on violent protest, direct action, and publicity to further their cause. They held processions, demonstrations and marches. They chained themselves to railings, smashed windows, invaded the House of Commons. At the front of their marches would be the figure of Flora Drummond. She came from the Isle of Arran, and had worked there in the telegraph station. Then she had moved to Manchester to work in a typewriter office, and had become a close friend of Christabel Pankhurst. Her friends called her 'The General', for she wore a kind of military uniform and rode on horseback at the head of suffragette processions.

The movement was growing in Scotland too. There were big demonstrations in Edinburgh in 1907, and in 1908 a Scottish headquarters of the Union was opened in Glasgow. Supporters came from all sorts of backgrounds. Janie Allan was one: her father and brother owned the Allan shipping line. Another was Helen Crawford, who later would be a founder of the Communist Party. Then there were the actresses Annie Fraser and Maggie Moffat. They were the first two Scots arrested during the campaign.

Flora Drummond being arrested in Hyde Park, London, in 1914

Despite all the activity, the government would do nothing. And so the Pankhursts stepped up their campaign. In 1909 Mrs Pankhurst was again arrested and sent to prison. This time she refused to eat any food. This tactic spread to Scotland, where suffragettes in Dundee went on hunger-strike. By 1912 tactics had become still more violent. Windows were smashed in the Dundee Inland Revenue Office and the Aberdeen Central Telephone Office. Pillar boxes across the country were filled with a sticky black fluid. 1913 saw a wave of fires deliberately started across the country. During the night of the 27th of April fires destroyed the grandstands at Kelso Racecourse and Ayr Racecourse. On the 3rd of May the Ashley Road School in Aberdeen was set alight. On the 10th of May Farrington Hall in Dundee was razed to the ground. On the 21st of May a bomb went off in Edinburgh's Blackford Observatory. The attack of the 'incendiarists' continued throughout that year: on Stair Park House, Tranent, on Leuchars Railway Station, on Fettes College, Edinburgh and Kelly House, Wemyss Bay.

Then in spring 1914 Mrs Pankhurst came to Glasgow to address a meeting at the St Andrews Hall. At the time, the police were after her under a law that the public nicknamed the Cat and Mouse Act. This act allowed suffragettes on hunger strike in prison to go free until they had recovered their strength. Then they were arrested again and taken back to prison. To avoid re-arrest Mrs Pankhurst was smuggled into St Andrews Hall in a laundry basket, but as soon as she started to speak to the packed hall the police charged the platform and arrested her. Amid scenes of furious anger and rioting she went back to prison yet again.

The tactics of the Pankhursts and their followers caused a lot of arguments at the time. Some people supported votes for women, but felt that the Pankhursts were going about it the wrong way. They felt that the hunger strikes, and the fire-raising, and the attacks on the Liberal government, did more harm than good, and put people off. They called themselves suffragists instead of suffragettes, and one of the most famous suffragists was Dr Elsie Inglis.

Elsie Inglis was born in 1864 while her parents were in the Himalayas, but came to Edinburgh to go to school. Then she trained to be a doctor in London and Dublin, before returning to Edinburgh in 1894 to start work. By 1900 she was as strongly in favour of votes for women as the Pankhursts or anyone else. 'A good New Year, and the vote *this* year', was the greeting she sent to all her friends at the end of each December. But she believed in working for this end through her job and through the Liberal Party.

In 1901 she started a small nursing-home in George Square, Edinburgh, and in 1904 she moved it to the High Street. There she could work amidst the slums helping working women look after themselves and their babies. It was Scotland's only maternity training centre run by women, and did a tremendous amount to help women. One of Edinburgh's maternity hospitals is still named in honour of her.

No-one will ever know if suffragettes or suffragists had the better tactics for winning the vote. For by August 1914 Britain was at war. The Pankhursts toured Britain speaking in favour of the war. Dr Elsie Inglis raised a medical team to help on the battlefields. Millions of women became a key part of the war effort, making shells, bombs, guns, and uniforms. And in January 1918, women were rewarded when the wartime government passed the Representation of People Act giving a vote to all women over 30 years of age. But for Elsie Inglis the new law was too late in coming, for she died just six weeks before her dream came true.

Medals awarded to Elsie Inglis for her medical work during the war

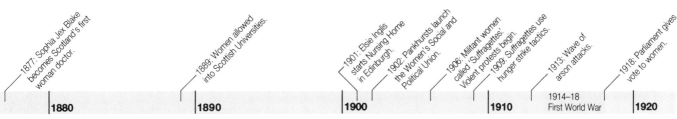

Votes for women: a time-line showing important events

1877: Sophia Jex Blake becomes Scotland's first woman doctor.

1889: Women allowed into Scottish Universities.

1901: Elsie Inglis starts Nursing Home in Edinburgh.

1902: Pankhursts launch the Women's Social and Political Union.

1906: Militant women called 'Suffragettes'. Violent protests begin.

1909: Suffragettes use hunger strike tactics.

1913: Wave of arson attacks.

1914–18 First World War

1918: Parliament gives vote to women.

1880   1890   1900   1910   1920

Keir Hardie and the Labour Party

After 1884, many men had to decide for the first time which political party to support with their vote.

But the Conservatives in Scotland were still thought by many to be the party of the landlords. And it seemed as if the Liberals didn't want to know about the problem of unemployment in the 1880s, far less do anything about it. And so working class support for the Liberals started to ebb. A new party began to appear, and to take the place of the Liberals. This was later to become the Labour Party, and the person who did as much as anyone to start it was a Scotsman called Keir Hardie.

Keir Hardie was born in 1856 near Holytown in Lanarkshire. By 1865, before he was nine years old, he was at work in the Glasgow shipyards, running messages, heating rivets, and doing any other job that was going. By 1866, aged 11, he was bringing home the family's main wage, working in a baker's shop from 7 in the morning until 7.30 at night.

One morning 11 year old Keir Hardie was 15 minutes late for work at the baker's shop because he had been up all night helping his mother nurse his brother, who had a bad fever. The master of the shop sent for him:

'I had never before seen such a beautiful room, nor such a table, loaded as it was with food and beautiful things. The master read me a lecture before the assembled family on the sin of slothfulness, and added that though he would forgive me for that once, if I sinned again by being late I should be instantly dismissed . . . Two mornings afterwards I was again a few minutes late, from the same source, and was informed on arriving at the shop that I was discharged and my fortnight's wages forfeited by way of punishment. The news stupefied me, and finally I burst out crying and begged the shopwoman to intercede with the master for me. The morning was wet and I had been drenched in getting to the shop and must have presented a pitiable sight as I stood at the counter in my wet patched clothes. She spoke with the master through a speaking tube, presumably to the breakfast room I remembered so well, but he was obdurate, and finally she, out of the goodness of her heart, gave me a piece of bread and advised me to look for another place. For a time I wandered about the streets in the rain, ashamed to go home where there was neither food nor fire, and actually discussing whether the best thing was not to go and throw myself in the Clyde and be done with a life that had so little attractions. In the end I went to the shop and saw the master and explained why I had been late. But it was all in vain. The wages were never paid.' Hardie would never forget this experience.

JAMES KEIR HARDIE, SOCIALIST AND LABOR LEADER.

Keir Hardie in America: a drawing in the *Chicago Tribune*, 1895. Hardie visited many parts of the world, spreading his views but also finding out how others thought and lived.

From Glasgow the family moved back to the coalfields and Hardie got a job as a miner. Then he moved to Ayrshire and in 1886 became the secretary of the Ayrshire Miners' Union. He was becoming more and more involved in the fight for better wages and conditions. He tried to become an M.P., but the Liberals would not support him and he was defeated. Then in 1892 he did manage to get into Parliament, as M.P. for West Ham in London. It was a sensational victory. The House of Commons was in an uproar when Hardie arrived wearing a cloth cap. Gladstone himself stared in amazement because Hardie wasn't dressed 'as a gentleman should be'. Not that the fuss bothered Hardie one whit. In fact he turned the publicity to his advantage. He spoke time and again in Parliament for the unemployed, the low paid, the sick, the badly housed, the ill-educated.

In 1893 Hardie was involved in setting up the Independent Labour Party. It was the first big step towards the Labour Party that exists today. Then in the 1906 election 50 Labour candidates stood for Parliament and 29 of them won. Only two of the winners were in Scotland, one in Dundee and the other in Glasgow, but it was another sign that the long run of the Liberals

VOTE FOR

Home Rule.

Democratic Government.

Justice to Labour

No Monopoly.

No Landlordism

Temperance Reform.

Healthy Homes.

Fair Rents.

Eight-Hour Day.

Work for the Unemployed.

KEIR HARDIE.

Printed and Published by F W. Scr sr & Co. [L S.C.], 151, Barking Road, Canning Town, London, E.

An election poster of 1895

in Scotland was coming to an end. Another unemployment crisis in 1908 pushed even more people away from the Liberals and towards Labour. In 1910 William Adamson became the first miner M.P. from West Fife. Abroad, too, Hardie was linking hands with others who shared his ideas. In Switzerland in 1913, Labour and Socialist parties from all over Europe met and agreed that the working classes of different countries should never fight each other in a war. Being working class, they thought, was more important than being British or French or German.

But it was not to be. War broke out in 1914, and most workers rushed to join up. Trade Unionists, Socialists, Labour councillors and Labour M.P.s almost all supported the war. Hardie's call for a general strike across Europe to stop the war was a voice in the wilderness. When he spoke at public meetings he was heckled and shouted down. His spirits were crushed and his heart broken, and he died in 1915. He was cremated in Maryhill, amidst much mourning and many tributes. Many of those present agreed with Sylvia Pankhurst: 'Keir Hardie' she said, 'has been the greatest human being of our time.'

Work to do . . .

1 When were the three great Reform Acts passed? To whom did they give the vote? Who were left without the vote after the Third Reform Act?
2 Write out the meaning of the following words and phrases: universal male suffrage; incendiarists; suffragettes; the 'Cat and Mouse Act'.
3 In your opinion, what effect did the Great War have on the campaign for votes for women? What reasons can you give for your view?
4 a When did Keir Hardie first become an M.P.? Why did he cause an uproar when he arrived at the House of Commons? Who did he speak up for in Parliament?
 b Why did Keir Hardie think that a war in Europe could be prevented? When the Great War broke out in 1914, how did he hope to end it?

51

The Great War

The Gathering Storm

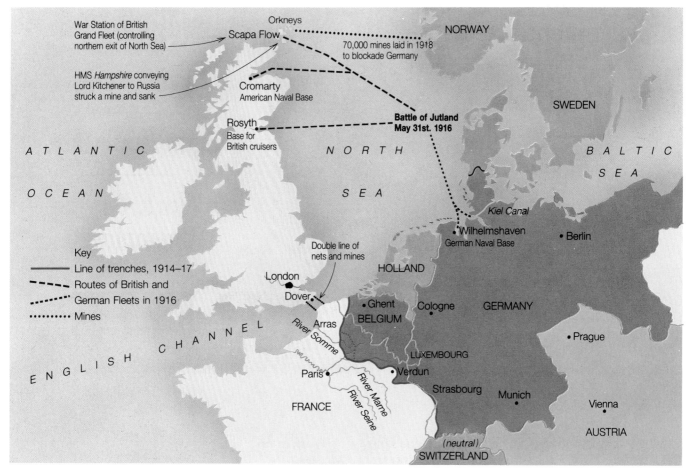

Key
— Line of trenches, 1914–17
- - - Routes of British and
German Fleets in 1916
· · · · · · Mines

War Station of British Grand Fleet (controlling northern exit of North Sea)

HMS *Hampshire* conveying Lord Kitchener to Russia struck a mine and sank

Orkneys
Scapa Flow
70,000 mines laid in 1918 to blockade Germany
NORWAY
SWEDEN

Cromarty
American Naval Base

Rosyth
Base for British cruisers

Battle of Jutland
May 31st. 1916

ATLANTIC
OCEAN

NORTH
SEA

BALTIC
SEA

Kiel Canal
Wilhelmshaven
German Naval Base
Berlin

Double line of nets and mines

HOLLAND

London
Dover

Ghent
BELGIUM
Cologne
GERMANY

Arras
River Somme

LUXEMBOURG
Prague

ENGLISH CHANNEL

Paris
Verdun
River Marne
River Seine
FRANCE
Strasbourg
Munich
Vienna

(neutral)
SWITZERLAND
AUSTRIA

A map of the Great War of 1914–1918

By 1914, Scotland had become one of the most prosperous countries in the world. Unemployment was very low, with less than two in every hundred workers out of a job. 1913 had been an all-time record year for Scottish shipbuilding. The Clyde alone had built more than all of Germany's shipyards put together. The population of Glasgow had just passed the magic figure of one million, and the city boasted that it was the 'second city of the Empire'.

But there were also serious problems. For a start, the wealth created by Scotland's industries was not shared out. Some people were very rich while others lived in poverty. This had led to unrest in the factories, to strikes and conflict. Industrial relations had become bitter and tense.

Government was becoming more difficult too. Socialist parties and trade unions were gaining support and demanding more say in things. Militant women were demanding the vote. The threat of violence hung in the air.

It was the same all over Britain, indeed all over Europe. Waves of unrest affected the whole continent.

In 1914 the storm broke. It began in a town called Sarajevo, which is in Yugoslavia nowadays but at that time was in Austro-Hungary. An assassin's bullet killed the heir to the Austro-Hungarian throne. In Scotland it must have seemed at the time like a minor event in a faraway place. But it set off a chain reaction that plunged all of Europe into war. Austro-Hungary blamed the assassination on its neighbour Serbia and declared war. Germany backed Austro-Hungary, Russia backed Serbia. Germany declared war on Russia. Russia's ally France prepared for war, and Germany declared war on France. Finally, on August the 4th, Britain declared war on Germany. The 'Triple Entente' of Britain, France and Russia faced the 'Triple Alliance' of Germany, Austro-Hungary and Italy.

'The Lamps are Going Out'

Europe had rushed headlong into war, and all over the continent there were scenes of cheering and jubilation. Scotland was no different. In Glasgow the Corporation Tramways asked for volunteers amongst their staff. Within a day 1100 men – 1 in 6 – had volunteered. The Highland Light Infantry battalion they formed became known as the 'Tramways Battalion'. Dozens of similar battalions nicknamed 'pals battalions' were raised all over Scotland.

The fishing villages of the North-East provided men for the Royal Navy. In October the 'Northern Scot' newspaper reported 'remarkable scenes at Buckie':

'Over 120 recruits for the Moray Firth Company of the Naval Brigade assembled in the Cluny Square under Lieutenant McLeod. . . . In presence of a crowd estimated at about 5,000 the men were photographed. A packet of cigarettes was presented to each man by the Town Council, after which the men formed fours and headed by the town band marched to the station by way of Low Street. The men were conveyed by splendid train, which left at 3.30 pm, and as the train moved slowly out of the station, a thunderous roar of cheering rent the air. The scene was the most remarkable of its kind ever witnessed in the town.'

It was the same story in the far north. Here is one description of reservists joining a Highland regiment in the winter of 1914:

'The men trickled in at most of the stations in Caithness, and they became more numerous as the train entered Sutherlandshire. As the short winter day closed in, snow began to fall; and, as the train wound through the valleys, all the houses were lit up, and the people stood at the doors waving torches and chanting a high-pitched battle song. Except for the railway, nothing was changed. It was thus all through the ages that the clans had mustered, and it was thus that the women, the grandfathers, and the children had sent their men to war.'

Top Army recruitment poster *Above* Scottish soldiers marching near the River Marne on the Western Front. The photo was taken in August of 1915.

Most people expected that the war would not last for long. 'It'll all be over by Christmas', they said. They were wrong. It lasted four years and three months, until November 1918. By then it had become known as the 'Great War', because the killing and destruction had been far greater than ever before. By then 10 million men had been killed.

After the Great War, it was not so easy to believe in progress, or in Europe, or in civilisation. For Scotland, and for everyone else too, the Great War was the end of an era. One of the most famous statements of that time was made by Britain's Foreign Secretary Sir Edward Grey, just after war was declared on Germany. He was standing by a window in the Foreign Office, looking out into London's evening darkness. A lamplighter was making his way along the street, putting out the gas street lamps. 'The lamps are going out all over Europe', said Sir Edward, 'we shall not see them lit again in our lifetime.' Looking back, we can see how right he was. Europe had entered a terrible darkness.

Stalemate at Sea

Right Part of the Grand Fleet at anchor in orderly lines, Scapa Flow *Below* 'Lord Kitchener Wants You'

Britain looked to the Royal Navy to win the war, and put faith in the Dreadnoughts. This brought Scotland into the thick of things, because the Royal Navy had decided that its safest war-time bases would be up the Scottish coast. When war began, Britain's Grand Fleet had already taken up its battle stations at Scapa Flow, a huge natural anchorage in Orkney with the North Sea on one side and the Atlantic on the other. But things got off to a bad start. In September 1914 three old British cruisers were sunk by a modern German weapon, a submarine or U-boat. Then in October a battleship hit a German mine and sank. Up in Scapa Flow the commander of the Grand Fleet, Sir John Jellicoe, became deeply alarmed. Scapa Flow had no protection against submarines. 'I wonder I can ever sleep at all', he said; 'Thank goodness the Germans imagine we have proper defences . . . otherwise there would be no Grand Fleet left now.' Perhaps the Germans were also worried about mines, torpedoes and submarines, because their High Seas Fleet sheltered in the German bases. The North Sea had become a no-man's sea.

Only once did the British and German Dreadnoughts clash, in May 1916 off the coast of Denmark. There were 250 ships present at this, the battle of Jutland, and 25 admirals. Both sides were terrified of torpedoes, and the stakes were so high that neither side was prepared to take risks. The thought looming large in Admiral Jellicoe's mind was that with one mistake he could 'lose the war in a day'.

After less than an hour the booming guns fell silent and both fleets scurried away from the smoke and confusion to their bases. 6000 British sailors had been killed and 14 ships sunk, while the Germans had lost about 2500 sailors and 11 ships. The Germans claimed a victory because they had lost fewer men and fewer ships. The British also claimed victory because the German fleet never again risked leaving its base during the war. But there was little celebration amongst the Grand Fleet when it arrived back at Scapa Flow.

A few days after the Battle of Jutland, Scapa Flow was at the centre of things again. This time the news concerned Lord Kitchener, the British secretary for war. Kitchener was hugely popular in Britain. He was the symbol of patriotism, and his face stared out from thousands of army recruiting posters. He had decided to visit Russia, an ally in need of encouragement, and the plan was to sail from Scapa Flow on board the cruiser *Hampshire*. The ship, however, had hardly got under way when suddenly it exploded off Marwick Head. It sank in 15 minutes and only 12 men survived. Lord Kitchener's body was never found. The country was stunned, and there was wild talk of sabotage and treachery. Probably the ship hit a mine. But money came in from the whole nation to erect some monument to Kitchener and the crew of the *Hampshire*. A stone tower called Kitchener's Memorial was built on the cliff-top at Marwick Head, and still stands there.

BRITONS

"WANTS" YOU

JOIN YOUR COUNTRY'S ARMY!

GOD SAVE THE KING

Reproduced by permission of LONDON OPINION

54

The Western Front

The soldiers were still waiting for fighting to begin when Christmas Day arrived in 1914. And along some parts of the Western Front opposing soldiers decided to get together for a celebration. One army Captain remembered how

'Scots and Huns were fraternizing in the most genuine possible manner. Every sort of souvenir was exchanged, addresses given and received, photos of families shown etc. . . . A German NCO with the Iron Cross started his fellows off on some marching tune. When they had done I set the note for 'The Boys of Bonnie Scotland where the Heather and the Bluebells Grow', and so we went on, singing everything from 'Good King Wenceslas' down to the ordinary Tommies' songs, and ended up with 'Auld Lang Syne', which we all, English, Scots, Irish, Prussians, Wurttembergers etc., joined in.'

The war at sea had not turned out the way experts had expected. New weapons like torpedoes, mines, and submarines had changed everything. On land it was the same story. The generals assumed that the war would be like previous ones: cavalry charges, fast-moving offensives, massed attacks. But barbed wire had become easy to make. And rapid-firing machine guns had been invented. Both these things made it much easier to defend than to attack. And so by November 1914 the opposing sides in Europe had come to a complete standstill. They were lined up face to face along a front that stretched all the way from the English Channel coast in Belgium across France to the borders of Switzerland. All along this line, the Germans on one side and the French and British on the other prepared their defences. They dug deep trenches, strung barbed wire in front of them, crouched behind their rifles and machine guns, and waited.

By 1915 life on the Western Front had turned into a shocking nightmare. The generals started a series of attacks. Each time the same thing happened. At regular intervals a whistle was blown, and a wave of men left their trenches and marched towards the enemy. As they picked their way through the barbed wire of no-man's land, the enemy machine guns had the easiest of targets. It was not war as anyone understood it. It was simply the mass slaughter of young men, and on a bigger scale than ever before in history.

In the first big British attack at Loos in September 1915, there were 60,000 British and 20,000 German casualties in just 11 days. In 1916 things were even worse. Sir Douglas Haig, an Edinburgh-born army commander, had been put in charge of the British army in France. He believed that a direct attack on the German trenches could succeed. All that was required was a giant barrage of gunfire followed by a human battering ram, a huge wave of infantry soldiers surging forward. The attack would take place near the valley of the River Somme, about a hundred miles north of Paris. 'I feel that every step in my plan has been taken with the Divine help', said Haig just before the attack. It began on the 1st of July 1916.

It was the worst day in the history of the British army. As the British soldiers rose to the sound of the whistles and went 'over the top' of their defences towards the Germans, the enemy machine-guns sprayed out a deadly hail of bullets. Before that day was out, 20,000 British soldiers had been killed and another 60,000 wounded. Haig stubbornly pressed his men on. The attack continued for days, weeks, months. It didn't stop until November, and then only because the whole area had become a sea of mud deep enough to drown in. By then, the number of casualties was almost too big to imagine: 420,000 British, 465,000 German, 200,000 French. A million men had been sacrificed for a few miles of farmland.

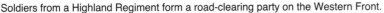
Soldiers from a Highland Regiment form a road-clearing party on the Western Front.

No-one knows exactly how many Scottish soldiers died during the Great War. Britain as a whole lost about 770,000 men, and probably about 110,000 of them were Scottish. Almost one in every three young men aged between 16 and 25 had been wiped out. Almost every family in the country had lost someone. In some villages and small towns, a complete generation had been killed. Parts of the Highlands were savaged. In Lewis, for example, out of a total population of 29,500, about 6,700 joined the forces. 1,151 of them died. Whole 'pals battalions' had died in the mud, like the Tramways Battalion at the Somme. All over the country, memorials started to appear, with the names of dead men and of the places where they had been killed: Loos, the Somme, Passchendaele, Ypres, Gallipoli, Mons.

Memories of the Great War

We can try to imagine what it was like to be a soldier in the Great War, but only those who were actually there can ever really know. Many of them, when they returned to Scotland, could not find the words to describe what they had been through. Some were 'shellshocked' and had mental breakdowns. Others became what we would call 'drop-outs'.

James Henderson was born in 1908 and spent his early life in the Borders. He can still remember meeting the ex-soldiers after the Great War:

'They were interesting men. I remember one fellow that I spoke to coming over Soutra one day, and he had been in the army in the First World War, he'd come of a good family, and he'd been in the army in the First World War, and I think it had slightly deranged him. I said to him were you demobbed in 1918? He said no, they kept me on. I said what were you doing? Oh, he said, I was clearing up the battlefields and making up the war cemeteries. And, when he came out, he had no stomach for going to any sort of trade, or profession, so he took to the road and he had a tin whistle, and he said, oh, I can do fine, I can go down to Melrose and the tourists coming off the train, and he says I'll play the whistle and I go round and put my hat out, I'll get some money. Then he said, people are very good they'll give you a lump of bread and butter with a lump of beef in it, and fill your can up with tea, and he said if the weather is fine you'll sleep at the back of a hedge, and if it's not so good you'll get into the barn . . . they were very common, believe me, there were any number of them wandering about the country.'

Other men returned to lives of work, but were full of hatred and contempt for war and all those who had played a part in running it.

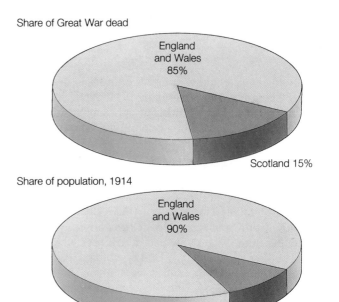

Share of Great War dead

England and Wales 85%

Scotland 15%

Share of population, 1914

England and Wales 90%

Scotland 10%

Above Casualties of the Great War
Below A war memorial at Sandbank, Argyll

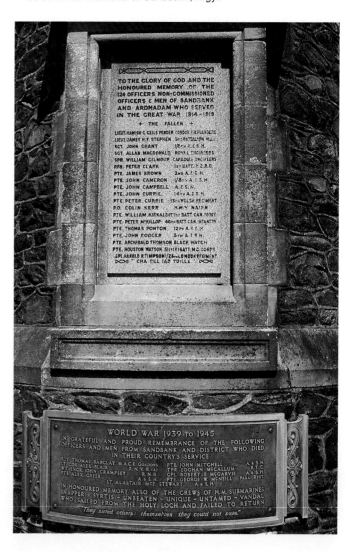

John Buchan, born in Perth in 1875, led a packed life as a publisher, journalist, writer, and politician. He later became Lord Tweedsmuir.

Like many other Scots, John Buchan lost many close friends during the Great War. 'There are far more dead than living now', he said in 1918. Towards the end of the war, he wrote a poem about a Scottish soldier daydreaming of peace back home with his friend Davie. Here's part of it:

We'll stop at the yett ayont the hicht
And drink great wauchts o' the scented nicht,
While the hoose lamps kin'le raw by raw
And a yellow star hings ower the law.

Davie will lauch like a wean at a fair
And nip my airm to mak certain shure
That we're back frae yon place o' dule and dreid,
To oor ain kind warld-

But Davie's deid!
Nae mair gude nor ill can betide him.
We happit him doun by Beaumont toun,
And the half o' my hert's in the mools aside him.

Vincent Flynn, who was born in West Kilbride in 1909, became friendly with a man called Alec Cochrane just after the Great War. Alec had always been mad about horses, and Vincent remembers that

'when war broke out he had volunteered, gone down to sign on and become a soldier, and his father went with him. His father, I always remember him telling me the story, when he came out his father says: "And what regiment have you joined?" "I don't know," he said, "but I've got a horse". And so he joined a regiment of horses called The Queen's Own Glasgow Yeomanry. He went out and he fought in the Allenby Campaign in the, you know, the Middle East, and from being an enthusiastic horseman and soldier he became a very bitter hater of everything to do with the military.'

And Vincent Flynn also remembers one way that Alec Cochrane found to show how much he hated war. In 1919 the government decided that as a mark of respect to those who had suffered and died there would be a two minute silence in the whole of Britain. Everything was to stop: no traffic, no machines, no moving, walking, talking; just silence. But when the silence began, Vincent remembers Alec, who worked as a bookbinder, picking up a hammer and beating away at the covering on a big leather book to bend it into shape.

'And I always remember the boss coming up. He was a young man, there was a father and two sons and the eldest son he ran the show, as the manager you know. He came rushing up. It's great to see how people meet people and meet situations. He came running up, sees it was Alec Cochrane, turns on his heels and away back, he couldn't say anything. He was just old enough maybe to have been in the army, but hadn't been in the army. And he knew that Alec Cochrane was . . . had been in the army, and had had his fill of soldiering. So he didn't dare challenge the man. But I thought what a reckless but splendid thing for a man to do, because he was putting his whole future, his job at risk.'

Work to do . . .

1 Describe in your own words the events leading up to the Great War, and the reaction of most people when war was declared.
2 Who was Sir John Jellicoe? Why was he a worried man by the end of 1914? Why was he cautious at the Battle of Jutland?
3 See if you can arrange a visit to your local war memorial.

Try to count the number of names of people killed during the Great War, and compare this with the number of names on the memorial for the Second World War of 1939–1945. If there are any place-names of Great War battlefields, make a note of them, then try to find them on the map at the beginning of this chapter.

The Home Front

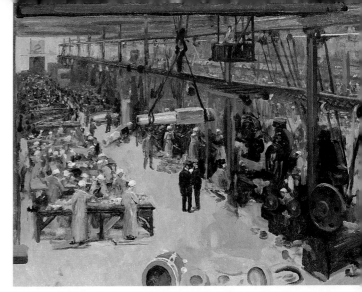

Inside a munitions factory. Painting by war artist, John Lavery

During the Great War the differences between soldiers and civilians started to disappear. The army relied completely on supplies pouring out of the factories. Gradually the whole country went to war. It became a war between British and German factories, British and German shipyards. Civilians became targets for attack. The British slowly starved the Germans by blockade. The Germans torpedoed merchant ships. Civilian life had turned into another part of the war effort: the 'Home Front' had come into being.

The Highlands at War

A heavy burden fell upon the Highlands. First, there was the Grand Fleet, stationed at Scapa Flow. The railway line from Perth through Inverness north to Wick suddenly became the Grand Fleet's vital artery. It almost broke under the strain, as thousands of extra trains rumbled back and forth carrying sailors, coal, ammunition and supplies. The strain on the life of Orkney, too, was heavy, for there were 20,000 sailors in the Grand Fleet.

There was another naval base at Invergordon on the Cromarty Firth. It jumped in size from one thousand people to almost eight thousand in a few years. In fact the whole Highland area became so important to naval operations that in 1916 the government declared it a 'restricted area'. North and west of the Great Glen became almost a separate country, where passes were needed to get in and out.

Fishing was more affected by the Great War than any other industry, and again the Highlands paid a high price. First there were the dangers of mines and U-boats. These sank 25 steam drifters off Shetland in a single night in 1915. In all, 90 boats were sunk off Scotland during the war. Many more boats stopped fishing and turned to new war tasks: as patrol boats, transports and a dozen other things. 'The Grand Fleet could not have existed without the trawlers' said the Admiral of the Fleet Lord Jellicoe. By 1918 almost 25,000 of Scotland's fishermen were involved in Royal Navy work.

U-boat attacks on Britain's imports had their own special effects in the Highlands. Imports of timber almost stopped and the saws had to be turned onto the Highland forests. The Canadian Forestry Corps gave a helping hand as the last swathes of the old Caledonian Pine Forest were felled. Even so, there were desperate shortages of wood by 1917. The supply of wooden pit props from Norway almost stopped, threatening the mines. The crisis passed, but it led the government to set up the Forestry Commission. In the future, it was hoped, Britain would not be short of timber even if there was another blockade.

Working for Victory

Between 1914 and 1918, almost all of Scotland was drawn further and further into the war effort. In Dundee, the jute industry produced vast amounts of sacking for the hundreds of millions of sandbags needed in the trenches. Scotland's textile industries also helped to equip the army with tents and groundsheets, tarpaulins and uniforms. Farmers all over the country somehow managed to produce more food, even though one third of the farmworkers had enlisted in the Army by 1918. New factories were opened, like the huge explosives works at Gretna near Carlisle.

Clydeside became the hub of Scotland's war effort. Here were the shipyards and forges, the great engineering works and engine shops, and the workers that could produce the tools of war. By 1917 a quarter of a million people were working on Clydeside in the munitions industries. The Clyde had become the biggest munitions centre in Britain.

Conditions in the munitions factories were often bad. People had to work long hours. More and more machines were crammed into factories, making work cramped and unpleasant. There was danger involved in making fuses, mines, shells, bombs and bullets.

Despite all these difficulties, there was very little trouble. Strikes during the Great War were four times less than they had been before it started, and ten times less than they were after it finished. Patriotism created peace in the factories, just as it created volunteers for the army. But there was trouble in Clydeside's engineering shops: not a lot, but enough to create a legend – the legend of 'the Red Clyde'.

LABOUR AFFAIRS.

CLYDE ENGINEERS' WAGES.

A STRIKE AT GLASGOW.

An unfortunate dispute at the works of Messrs G. and J. Weir, Cathcart, Glasgow, resulted yesterday in a strike of the engineers employed by that firm. The men first asked that their wages should be increased by 6s per week in order to bring their rates up to the level of those which, they alleged, were paid to certain American workmen in the firm's employment. Later it was stated that the men were on strike in order to enforce their demand for an advance of 2d per hour. The matter has been reported to the Executive Council of the Amalgamated Society of Engineers, who are expected to endeavour to-day to negotiate for a settlement.

Newspaper story from February 1915

The Red Clyde

The strike created a tremendous fuss. The press was in a very powerful position during the Great War, for there was no radio or television to provide other sources of information. And the press was very hostile to the strikers. They accused them of being traitors, of being paid 'German gold'. They printed poems, like 'Tommy Atkins at the Front', in which Tommy throws down his rifle in disgust when he hears about the strike. Then he decides that he has to fight on, and tells of how he 'picked up me old gun; me bit of iron, too: I'm jist a common soldier so I've got to see it through. An' if they lets us down at 'ome, and if 'e reads I died, will 'e know 'e 'elped to kill me – my brother on the Clyde?'

The biggest problem in the engineering shops of Clydeside was the skilled craftsmen. These were men who had served a long apprenticeship learning their trade, and who were proud of their skills as fitters or turners. They were the elite of the working class, earning twice as much as unskilled men. They had fought long and hard for their position, and guarded it jealously against their employers and against other workers.

Usually, the employers were happy with this situation. Skilled men were nearly always in short supply, and firms liked to hold onto their own skilled workers. But one or two employers wanted change. Amongst them was William Weir, who was to be one of the main figures on the Clyde during the Great War.

In 1910 William Weir had taken charge of his father's engineering company, which specialized in making pumps. William travelled widely on business: in 1911–12 he went round the world. He saw how ruthless and efficient American industry was. He became convinced that unless Scottish industry changed its ways, it would be wiped out by foreign competition.

Weir's first efforts were not very successful. The engineers had been asking for a rise of tuppence an hour since before the war started. Everything seemed to be going up in price once war was declared, and they felt their claim for a rise was reasonable. By the end of 1914 they were losing patience, and made a threat to stop work unless they got more pay. Weir, however, refused to listen. He argued that the engineers should tear up all their old 'who does what' agreements. He published a pamphlet attacking them: 'every hour lost by a workman which COULD HAVE been worked, HAS been worked by a German workman, who in that time has produced, say, an additional shell . . . to kill the British workman's brother-in-arms, or perhaps a bomb to be dropped on his wife and children.'

This caused a lot of anger amongst the skilled engineers. And they became even angrier when Weir brought over a squad of American engineers and paid them the money he was refusing to pay the Scottish engineers. The final straw came when 150 skilled engineers were brought up from England to ease the shortages at the huge Parkhead works of Beardmore's. By February 1915 the engineers were on strike all over Clydeside. The 'tuppence an hour strike' had begun.

With the press against them, and the public against them, and even their own union against them, the engineers found it hard to stay out on strike. Within a fortnight they had settled for an extra penny an hour and the 'tuppence an hour' strike was over. Compromise had won the day, and the first episode of 'Red Clydeside' was over.

Rent Strike

Right Many of the rent strikers in 1915 were women whose husbands were in the army. The photograph shows women and children holding a demonstration during the strike. *Below* Lloyd George, Minister of Munitions, on a visit to Glasgow in 1915.

Another source of unrest on Clydeside during 1915 was housing. So many extra munitions workers were arriving in Glasgow that housing became scarce. So some landlords tried to push up rents, and to evict people who resisted. Over the summer, more and more people decided to go on a rent strike in protest. It began in Partick, then spread to Govan. Soon about 20,000 people were refusing to pay their rent.

Support for the rent strikers grew, but in October 1915 it looked as if evictions might begin. At this point workers in the big engineering factories stepped in. They would come out on strike, they said, if anyone was evicted. Immediately, the government stopped anyone from being evicted and passed new laws to control rents. Another strike on Clydeside was over, and this time the strikers had won.

Dilution

As 1915 drew on, unrest continued in the engineering works of Clydeside. The main cause of the trouble was 'dilution', the use of unskilled workers to do work normally done by skilled men.

At the end of 1915 David Lloyd George, the government's Minister of Munitions, decided to come to Glasgow to try to stop the unrest. He was well-known as a brilliant speaker who could sway an audience with his dramatic performances. People sometimes called him the Welsh Wizard.

The main event was a big meeting at the St Andrew's Hall on Christmas Day. Three thousand workers packed in.

When Lloyd George entered the hall, there was pandemonium. A choir started to sing 'See the Conquering Hero Comes'. The audience replied by singing

'The Red Flag'. When he tried to speak, there were constant booings, hissings, and heckling. Eventually the meeting finished in chaos, and a few days later Lloyd George left Glasgow.

Peace in the Factories

Lloyd George had lost the day, but he had won the battle. David Kirkwood, a union shopsteward at the giant Parkhead works of Beardmore's, seemed to realise this: 'I had seen Lloyd George face to face. He was not the kind of man to be put off his stride by a rowdy meeting . . . It was the first time that a Cabinet Minister had come to the people informally, to talk to them man to man. He had taken a big risk to make peace with us, and we had given him a sword with which to smite us.' A few weeks after the St Andrew's Hall fiasco, in January 1916, Lloyd George acted. He appointed three commissioners to introduce dilution on Clydeside as quickly as possible.

Their work went very smoothly. They went from factory to factory drawing up agreements with the owners and the unions. Between January and April 1916 they held 1000 factory conferences. The only big problem arose at Beardmore's Parkhead works. There, the managers broke the agreement they had made with the workers. A strike began at the end of March 1916. It spread quickly to other factories. The government broke the strike by having the main shop stewards at Parkhead arrested. David Kirkwood was arrested at home at three o'clock in the morning by four detectives carrying revolvers. The strike-leaders were deported to Edinburgh, and the strike collapsed.

After that strike, there was hardly any more trouble on Clydeside during the war. Even the jailed strike leaders like David Kirkwood and William Gallacher were soon making munitions again.

'What a team!' Kirkwood later boasted; 'There never was anything like it in Great Britain. We organised a bonus system in which everyone benefited by high production. Records were made only to be broken. In six weeks we held the record for output in Great Britain, and we never lost our premier position.' David Lloyd George, the Welsh Wizard, also had good reason to be pleased. He had been so successful as Minister of Munitions that by December 1916 he was Prime Minister.

The End of the War

Throughout 1917 and 1918, war materials poured out of Scotland's munitions industries. There were new weapons too. Hundreds of torpedoes came from a new factory in Greenock. Beardmore's and Weir's in Glasgow produced about 2000 aircraft between them in the last years of the war. At the Heathhall works at Dumfries, two and a half thousand people were at work building aero engines. These new weapons started to change the shape of the war, to break the stale-mate in the trenches.

A turning point came in 1917. The Americans, stung by German U-boat attacks on their ships, declared war on Germany. Soon Rosyth was welcoming a new fleet of warships, ships with names like *U.S.S. Texas*, and *U.S.S. Delaware*.

Germany, well aware of the huge strength of American industry, tried to push for a victory before America was too deeply involved. Attack after attack was launched on the French and British trenches. Extra German troops arrived from the Russian Front. There, the strains of the war had created the conditions for the Russian revolution. By October 1917 Lenin's Bolsheviks had seized power, and by spring 1918 had signed a peace treaty with Germany. But even the extra help arriving from the east did not lead to German victory on

Painting by J. D. Fergusson of ships being repaired, 1918

During the Great War, Scotland's artists produced some fine work. They were encouraged by the government, which appointed many of Britain's best painters as official war artists. And so J.D. Fergusson joined the Royal Navy in 1918 and produced some of the most original paintings of his career, including unusual images of naval dockyards and ships being repaired. James McBey travelled all over Egypt, Lebanon and the Middle East making dozens of drawings of the British Army. And John Lavery was at work throughout the war, painting the first wounded soldiers arriving in London from the Front in 1914, and the surrender of the German Fleet at Rosyth in November 1918.

the Western Front. By summer of 1918 another one million German soldiers were dead, wounded or taken prisoner. German resistance began to falter, and a peace delegation headed west for talks with the Allies.

And so, at 11 am on the 11th day of the 11th month of 1918, the Great War came to an end.

In Scotland, and all over Britain, the news was greeted with a tremendous surge of relief. The long years of slaughter were over.

Work to do . . .

1 Explain in your own words the meaning of the phrase the 'Home Front'.
2 What effect did the Great War have upon: Scotland's fishing industry; the Highland railways; the forests?
3 Draw up a list of events that helped to create the image of 'Red Clydeside'. Then say in a few sentences whether you think that the image was accurate, giving your reasons.
4 Write out the meaning of these words and phrases: munitions industries; blockade; rent strike; dilution; the Welsh Wizard.

A Workshop without Work

A Fit Country for Heroes

Hardly had the Armistice with Germany been signed when Britain's war-time Prime Minister, Lloyd George, called a general election. He wanted to keep together the war-time coalition of political parties, but the Labour Party, still young and small, decided to oppose him.

Lloyd George's supporters stomped round the country making promises. Abroad, it was promised that Germany would be treated sternly: 'We will get everything out of her that you can squeeze out of a lemon and a bit more' said the First Lord of the Admiralty, the Edinburgh-born Sir Eric Geddes; 'I will squeeze her until you can hear the pips squeak.' At home, the most famous promise was made by Lloyd George himself: 'What is our task? To make Britain a fit country for heroes to live in.'

When voting took place in December 1918, Lloyd George's Coalition won a huge victory. Scotland voted much the same as the rest of Britain, and only 7 of Scotland's 74 Members of Parliament belonged to the opposition Labour Party. Lloyd George had steered the country to victory in war; now people were giving him the chance to 'finish the job'.

The Red Clydeside Again?

One of the first problems that Lloyd George's new government had to deal with was on Clydeside at the beginning of 1919. There, trade unionists had been worried that men pouring out of the armed forces back into civilian life might face mass unemployment. So they had been calling for a big reduction in hours worked, to 40 hours a week, in order to share the work around. When Lloyd George was elected, they decided to hold a strike to press their claim.

The 'Forty-Hour Strike' began on January 27th 1919. There were strikes up and down Britain, but the main places affected were Edinburgh, Belfast and especially Glasgow. 40,000 people were on strike in Glasgow on the first day, and by the next day the number had almost doubled. Things reached a climax on Friday 31st, when a huge crowd gathered in Glasgow's George Square to find out if the unions and government had reached any agreement.

Amidst the milling crowds, the police failed to 'keep the heid'. They suddenly mounted a baton charge to clear the tramlines. In the confusion, two trade union leaders, William Gallacher and Emmanuel Shinwell, were arrested. A third leader, David Kirkwood, was cracked on the head with a baton as he ran out of the Council Chambers to see what was happening.

George Square, Glasgow, January 31st 1919

A police panic had cleared George Square. Press photos revealed Bolshevik flags fluttering above the sea of cloth caps. With the Russian Revolution of 1917 still fresh in the mind – and strike leaders like Gallagher well-known as supporters of the Bolsheviks – the government reacted. By Saturday the 1st of February 12,000 troops had been rushed to Glasgow, six tanks were installed in the Cattle Market, and machine-gun nests had appeared in the city centre.

William Gallacher later wrote his account of the 1919 Forty-Hour Strike. In his view, Glasgow was on the very brink of a revolution. Revolution had not happened, but only because leaders like himself had not realised how close it was:

'Had we been capable of planning beforehand, or had there been an experienced revolutionary leadership of these great and heroic masses, instead of a march to Glasgow Green there would have been a march to Maryhill Barracks. For while troops, mostly young new recruits, with tanks, machine-guns and barbed wire were being brought forward for the encirclement of Glasgow, the soldiers of Maryhill were confined to barracks and the barrack gates were kept tightly closed. If we had gone there we could easily have persuaded the soldiers to come out and Glasgow would have been in our hands . . .

A rising was expected. A rising should have taken place. The workers were ready and able to effect it; *the leadership had never thought of it.*'

Although some members of the government would have agreed, a lot of the evidence was against Gallacher. Unrest did not continue.

But the next day the streets were quiet and many strikers were at football matches. Emmanuel Shinwell remembers the troops that had been drafted into the city being offered cups of tea and chatting with locals. Within days the strikers had returned to work on a 48-hour week. Clydeside was quiet.

February 1919, and tanks wait in Glasgow's Cattle Market in case of serious trouble. They were not needed. The pile of kitbags on the ground suggests that they have just arrived.

Boom and Slump

One reason why the Forty-Hour Strike did not last was that there was very little unemployment in 1919. Many men leaving the army took the jobs that women had been doing during the war. The women went back into the home, and by 1921 the number of women in paid jobs in Scotland was lower than before the war.

Unemployment was also kept low by a booming economy. People were spending their war-time savings, and companies began to invest in schemes for the future. It was a bumper year for shipbuilding, with over 650,000 tons launched on the Clyde. But in the winter of 1920, the boom collapsed.

For Scotland's industries, that winter signalled the start of long years of trouble. Almost everything had gone wrong. Shipbuilding was a good example. During the Great War countries like America, Japan and Sweden had expanded their own yards, either because they too were in the war, or because they could no longer get the ships they normally ordered on the Clyde. Now there were too many yards chasing too few orders. On top of that, there wasn't much trade to carry by ship. Germany had been a big trading partner of Britain before the war, but now she was being squeezed 'until the pips squeaked'. Her economy was in ruins. For Scotland, reliant on exports, things could hardly have been worse. The bottom had fallen out of Clyde shipbuilding: in 1923 only 170,000 tonnes were launched, a quarter of the tonnage launched in 1920. It was the same story in steel, coal, locomotives, and textiles. By 1922 unemployment in Scotland was soaring: that year 80,000 were without work in Glasgow alone. Hard times had arrived.

The Twenties

The end of the boom was also the end of Lloyd George, who was defeated in a general election in 1922. Britain couldn't agree who should take his place, or what should be done, and there were another three changes of government in the next two years. But the Scottish voters were beginning to back Labour more strongly than voters elsewhere in Britain. In 1922, 29 of the 74 Scottish MPs who were elected were Labour.

Labour did best in Glasgow, winning ten of the fifteen seats there. These 'Clydesiders', as they were called, included some famous left-wingers, like John Wheatley, James Maxton, David Kirkwood and Emmanuel Shinwell.

The Clydesiders did make some changes, but not as many as they or their supporters had expected. Like almost everyone else at the time, they had no detailed plan for solving Scotland's problems. Indeed, it was much harder at the time to see what the problems were than it is now, looking back. The fact is, there was no *single* problem. Scotland's industries had grown together before the Great War. It had been an upward spiral of success, with each industry helping and reinforcing others. Now it had turned into a downward spiral of decline, where each industry's failures damaged and weakened other industries. The shipbuilding yards had empty order books because of the lack of trade around the world, and this affected engineering companies. And because they were damaged, the forges and steel works suffered. And because they suffered, the coal mines were hit.

There were also too many small companies in Scotland competing with each other, none of them big enough to invest in modern efficient equipment and

James Maxton, a 'Red Clydesider', painted by John Lavery

The Clydesiders were given a terrific send-off in Glasgow as they prepared to take their places in Westminster. 8,000 people packed St Andrew's Hall to hear their promises. 'Don't hurry for the train' shouted James Maxton as they made their way to St Enoch Station, 'It'll all belong to the people when we come back.' When they arrived at Westminster, David Kirkwood said to John Wheatley 'John, we'll soon change all this.'

methods. It would have been better if they had grouped together. But the companies were not used to co-operating, and the workers resisted change.

A few things were done to prepare for the future. For instance, in 1924 William Weir the industrialist was asked by the government to find ways of improving the country's electricity industry. Britain's electrical supply was a shambles: voltages varied from town to town, and at least 23 different types of plug were in use! Weir went to work with his usual impatient gusto, and came up with a radical plan. The government should build a national network or 'grid' of power lines, from the north of Scotland to the south of England. The plan was accepted, and by 1931 a Central Scottish Grid had been built. The country was ready to 'hook up' new factories wherever they wanted to be.

Perhaps the government could have helped other industries as it helped the electricity industry. But it didn't, and Scotland staggered through the 1920s. During these years, an average of one Scottish worker in every seven was unemployed. Emigration soared to record levels, as almost 400,000 Scots decided to leave the country. This flood of emigration was so strong that Scotland's population actually fell during the 1920s for the first time since the industrial revolution. And still the gloom deepened.

An overturned bus during the General Strike of 1926. The trade unions called the strike to support the miners, but stopped it after 9 days.

NOTICE

Exceptional Chance for Lewis Girls
FOR
Domestic Service in Canada.

MISS YOUNG OF THE COLONIZATION DEPARTMENT OF THE CANADIAN PACIFIC RAILWAY COMPANY, will be at the undermentioned Centres in Lewis for the purpose of interviewing girls who may desire to go to Canada next Spring. The Girls will be accompanied from Stornoway to Montreal and Toronto where they will be placed in situations.

Miss Young who has for many years been connected with this work will give reliable information and guarantee situations.

TUESDAY, 10th December,	AIRD PUBLIC SCHOOL,		6—7.30 p.m.
"	BAYBLE "	"	8—9.30 p.m.
WEDNESDAY, 11th Dec.,	LIONEL "		6—7.30 p.m.
"	CROSS "	"	8—9.30 p.m.
THURSDAY, 12th Dec.,	CARLOWAY "		7—8.30 p.m.
	SHAWBOST "		9—10 p.m.
FRIDAY, 13th Dec.,	BACK "	"	7.30—9 p.m.

HOSTEL TRAINING FOR LEWIS GIRLS AT LENZIE, GLASGOW.

In connection with this Scheme—
SUPPORTED BY Mr. T. B. MACAULAY,
Miss Young will receive applications and interview intending applicants.

All Women interested in this scheme are cordially invited.

FULL INFORMATION CAN BE OBTAINED FROM
MURDO MACLEAN,
46 Point Street, Stornoway.

30th Nov., 1929.

A 1929 poster encouraging girls from Lewis to emigrate.

The Thirties

The 1920s had not been lean years everywhere. In America they were known as the Roaring Twenties. Giant new industries appeared in America, mass-producing things like refrigerators and cars. Some of this new wealth had spread to Scotland: new liners built mainly to carry wealthy Americans across the Atlantic had helped the Clyde through the 1920s.

By 1929 many Americans had begun to think that business was bound to keep on booming. Confidence in the future turned into a kind of euphoric madness. People began to believe that they could make fortunes out of nothing, by buying and selling shares on the stock exchanges. Wall Street, America's main stock exchange in New York, was gripped by the fever. Then suddenly, on October 24th 1929, the bubble burst. Share prices tumbled, and people, banks and companies went bankrupt by the thousand. The Wall Street Crash pushed America into an abyss, and soon it was in the worst economic depression in history.

The Crash echoed around the world. Some countries, like Germany, were affected more quickly and more deeply than others. But no country escaped. Without American orders, Britain's industries were soon in serious trouble. And Scotland, with so many industries that relied on exports, was hit especially badly. Twelve per cent of Scotland's workforce were jobless in 1929, but by 1930 the figure had jumped to 18 per cent, and by 1931 to 28 per cent. Scotland had been plunged into the Hungry Thirties.

The 1930s were years of despair for much of Scotland. Unemployment, poverty and decay spread throughout the country. When the Orcadian writer Edwin Muir journeyed through Lanarkshire in 1933, he was reminded of the Highland clearances:

'A century ago there was a great clearance from the Highlands which still rouses the anger of the people living there. At present, on a far bigger scale, a silent clearance is going on in industrial Scotland, a clearance not of human beings, but of what they depend upon for life . . . the surroundings of industrialism remain, but industry itself is vanishing like a dream.'

Later, in Glasgow, Muir went to see the shipyards:

'The weather had been good for several weeks, and all the men I saw were tanned and brown as if they had just come back from their summer holidays. They were standing in the usual groups, or walking by twos and threes, slowly, for one felt as one looked at them that the world had not a single message to send them on, and that for them to hasten their steps would have meant a sort of madness. Perhaps at some time the miracle of work glimmered at the extreme horizon of their minds; but one could see by looking at them that they were no longer deceived by such false pictures.'

American newspaper headlines during the Wall Street Crash of 1929

Scottish women on a march to London in February 1934. 'Hunger marches' like this became popular in the 1930s. They were held by communities gripped by the Depression, as a way of protesting against government policies. The most famous was the Jarrow Crusade of 1936.

Comings and Goings

In the 1920s a record number of Scots had emigrated. Although Scotland's plight was even worse in the 1930s, there was less emigration, because things were as bad elsewhere. In fact some people came back.

> Abe Moffat was born in Lumphinnans in Fife in 1921, and in 1923 his family moved to America. But when the Depression came in 1929, his father found it more and more difficult to get work:
>
> 'I can remember goin' with my mother and father into Newark, that's in New Jersey, that's a city, and seeing people livin' in the park, that there was no accommodation for them . . . they stood in the breadline and they got a bowl o' soup and a bit o' bread . . . Things were really getting desperate and my father, he walked all the way from Lyndhurst to Newark, and from Newark across to New York lookin' for jobs and couldn't get them. And he came in, his feet was raw with walkin'.' So Abe Moffat's father brought the family back from America to Fife in 1932.

Still, about 100,000 people left Scotland during the 1930s.

The government encouraged people to move, but left the decision to individuals or families. But in 1932 a whole community moved south. Stewarts and Lloyds were a steel tube-making company, whose works were at Mossend in Monklands near Glasgow. They were finding it increasingly difficult to get steel supplies in Scotland. So they decided to move, lock, stock and barrel, to a new site on top of the iron ore fields of Corby in Northamptonshire. Almost all their workforce moved south with them, and so a whole Scottish town came into being, just 80 miles north of London. To this day, more than 50 years later, Scottish accents are common in Corby, although the steel works is now closed.

The south and midlands of England were the main destination for most of the people who left Scotland in the 1930's. These areas didn't depend on heavy industry and exports. Instead, they had become centres for the new industries, making motor cars and household electrical goods like vacuums, fridges and radios. As a result, unemployment in London was only 6 per cent by 1936. In Scotland that year it was still around 19 per cent, and in places like Airdrie it was 30 per cent. Scotland's failure to attract the new industries was becoming very obvious and very costly.

Scottish and total United Kingdom unemployment rates between the wars

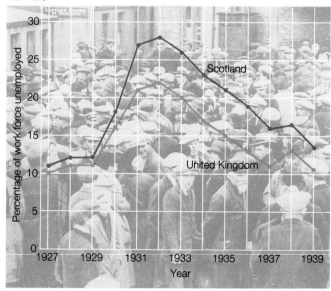

National Solutions?

Scotland's problems between the wars made some people question the union with England. Scotland had become a part of Britain with special difficulties. But there was no Scottish way of dealing with the problems. Power lay in London. Indeed, Scottish control of Scotland seemed to be shrinking rapidly: the railways, many of the banks, and parts of other industries had been taken over by English companies during the 1920s.

The same issues were bothering other parts of Britain. Ireland left the United Kingdom in 1921 amidst much trouble and bitterness. In 1925 a Welsh nationalist party called Plaid Cymru was formed. Then in 1928 the National Party of Scotland was formed at a meeting in Stirling. A few years later, in 1934, it joined forces with another party called the Scottish Party, and the Scottish National Party was born.

National feeling was running high in Scotland during the 1930s. It was decided to set up separate Scottish versions of national bodies like the National Trust and the Youth Hostel Association. Most of the government offices that dealt with Scotland were moved from London to new headquarters at St. Andrew's House in Edinburgh. And in 1938 a great Empire Exhibition was held in Glasgow to promote all that was best in Scotland.

But the Scottish National Party made little progress in Scotland between the wars. They argued a lot amongst themselves. Some wanted to be more left-wing, some to be more right-wing. Some wanted complete independence, others just a bit of Home Rule. But they also failed to offer any plan to deal with Scotland's economic problems. How would they deal with unemployment, declining industries, and lack of world trade? It was an international crisis as well as a local one.

So the 1930s were bad times for the Scottish National Party. When it was formed in 1934 it had 10,000 members, but by 1939 only 2,000.

Tait's Tower soaring above the Empire Exhibition, held in Bellahouston Park in the summer of 1938. It rained almost every day that summer, but over 13 million people passed through the gates to see the Pavilions and amusement parks, the Crazy House and roller coaster and much more. The Tower was named after the architect Thomas Tait who designed it.

Ramsay MacDonald and his family

The Nationalists were not the only party unsure what to do about the Great Depression. A Labour government had been elected just a few months before the Wall Street Crash. In 1931 it ran into a financial crisis. It seemed that confidence could be restored only by raising taxes and cutting government spending. Unemployment benefit would have to be cut, as would the pay of teachers, civil servants, the police and the armed forces.

The Prime Minister was Ramsay MacDonald. He came from Lossiemouth on the Moray coast. He had been one of the founders of the Labour Party. He was prepared to make the cuts that seemed necessary. But his Labour colleagues couldn't agree. Some backed him, others rejected a cut in unemployment benefit, and some rejected any cuts. Amidst a growing panic, MacDonald was forced to resign in August 1931, and become head of a National government supported by Conservatives, Liberals and a few Labour MPs.

MacDonald's actions caused great bitterness in the Labour Party. He was accused of betraying the Labour Party in order to remain Prime Minister. He was expelled from the party he had helped to create. He

replied that there had been a crisis and the Labour government had run away from it.

Whatever people might think now of Mac-Donald's actions, at the time he was given support. In the general election of October 1931, MacDonald asked the country to give his National government a 'doctor's mandate', a free hand to do what seemed necessary. He won the biggest victory in British election history: over 500 National government MPs, against just over 50 Labour. In Scotland, there had been 36 Labour MPs in 1929, but in 1931 the number fell to 7. MacDonald, the 'Moray Loon', was in charge.

Ship No. 534

Despite its huge majority, MacDonald's National government did not take any radical steps to deal with the Depression. It put taxes on imports, which helped the new industries of southern England but did nothing for Scotland's industries. Maybe the prosperity in the south and the size of the government's majority helped it to think that urgent action was not necessary.

January 1932, and long queues form outside the Clydebank Unemployment Exchange after work comes to a halt on the *Queen Mary*

One MP who tried constantly to shake the government into action was David Kirkwood. He was one of the handful of Labour MPs elected in Scotland in 1931. His constituency was Clydebank, home of John Brown's shipyard.

In 1930 work had begun there on a new super-liner for Cunard. She was planned to be the biggest and fastest liner in the world, weighing 81,000 tons, almost 300 metres long, and able to cross the Atlantic in four and a half days. She was ship number 534 for the yard, and that's what the men called her.

But in 1931 Cunard ran out of money, and the 3,000 men working on the liner were made idle. The abandoned hull towered over Clydebank. 'It seems to me to shout "failure, failure" to the whole of Britain' said Kirkwood. He did everything he could to get work restarted. So did Cunard and John Brown and William Weir. The King was taken to Clydebank by Kirkwood, and shown the effects of the halt. The Chancellor was pestered constantly. Finally in 1934 the government agreed to give a special loan, and work restarted on the 534. She was launched as the *Queen Mary* in 1935 and finished in 1936. By then, work was beginning on a sister ship, the *Queen Elizabeth*.

There were some other signs of action too. In 1934 the government made central Scotland one of four 'Special Areas' in Britain, where economic problems were specially bad, and where new light industries would be helped. As a result, the Hillington industrial estate west of Glasgow was opened in 1937.

But it was government action of a different kind that was beginning to ease Scotland's Depression. In one of his last acts as Prime Minister before retiring due to illness, MacDonald approved a new policy in the spring of 1935. It marked the moment when Britain decided it would have to start rearming because of the growing German threat. By 1936 rearmament had begun. By 1939 only £4 million had been spent on the 'Special Area' projects, but £80 million had poured into the Clyde shipyards on naval orders alone. Rearmament had come to the rescue of Scotland's heavy industries.

Work to do . . .

1 Explain in your own words the title of this chapter.
2 What was the 'Forty-Hour Strike' about? How did it end?
3 Imagine you were in George Square, Glasgow, on the 31st of January 1919. Now write a report of what you witnessed and how you felt.
4 Write ten lines describing emigration from Scotland during the 1920s and 1930s.
5 When was the Scottish National Party born? Would you say that its first years were successful or not? Explain your answer.
6 Who was Ramsay MacDonald? Why did some people accuse him of betraying the Labour Party? What verdict did the voters give in 1931?

Homes and Pleasure Domes

'Clotted Masses of Slums'

'What is our task? To make Britain a fit country for heroes to live in.' That was the election promise of Prime Minister Lloyd George at the end of 1918. If the promise was to be kept, big improvements would be needed in the country's health services and schools. But for Scotland in particular, one problem towered above all others: housing.

The Glasgow rent strike of 1915 had made Lloyd George aware of some of Scotland's housing problems. Then in 1917 a Royal Commission appointed by the government to examine the state of Scotland's housing published its report. It made shocking reading.

The Royal Commission found bad conditions everywhere:

'unspeakably filthy privy-middens in many of the mining areas, badly constructed incurably damp labourers' cottages on farms, whole townships unfit for human occupation in the crofting counties and islands, ... gross overcrowding and huddling of the sexes together in the congested industrial villages and towns, occupation of one-room houses by large families, groups of lightless and unventilated houses in the older burghs, clotted masses of slums in the great cities.'

It showed very clearly that housing was far worse in Scotland than in England. Half of all Scottish families were living in houses that had only one or two rooms, whereas only one in twelve English families lived in such small houses. The question was, how should the problem be tackled? The report's answer was clear: there would have to be a massive building programme, and it couldn't be left solely to private builders. The government would have to take responsibility for raising money to build the houses, and then get local councils to build and look after them.

The Dawn of the Council House Era

Glasgow set up a Council Housing Department in 1919, and began to build houses. These first council housing 'schemes' were meant to be as different as possible to the crowded slums. They were built on fresh green land away from the smoky pollution of the city centre. Many of the houses were semi-detached, or even terraced cottages. There was lots of space between them. Knightswood, built to the northwest of Glasgow between Partick and Clydebank in the years from 1923 to 1929, was a show-piece scheme, with a library, a social centre, and seven shopping 'parades'.

The schemes built in the 1930s were very different. They were built on the cheap. In Glasgow, the typical scheme of the 1930s was Blackhill, a thousand houses of three and four storey tenements. In Edinburgh, Wardieburn, Craigmillar and Pilton were built during the same period.

The new policy of building council houses marked a big break with the past. Before 1914, only one in a hundred families in Scotland had been housed by the local councils. The basic idea was to build houses and rent them to better-off working class families, whose old houses would then be free for people in the worst slums to move into. And so the slums would gradually empty and could be knocked down.

The first council houses were high quality and popular. But they were expensive. And people in slums just couldn't afford to move into the houses left empty by the new council house tenants. So in the 1930s councils began to tackle the slum problem directly, by clearing the slums and building big council schemes to replace them. These new houses were built as cheaply as possible, to keep rents low and put up as many as could be afforded. They were crammed onto poor land near railway lines and gasworks. There were none of the shopping parades, social centres, or terraced cottages that had been built in the 1920s.

This new policy in the 1930s certainly meant that a lot more houses were built. But almost as soon as they were finished, schemes like Craigmillar and Blackhill were notorious. In some ways they were even worse than the old slums. The lack of shops or facilities created a bleak, brutal environment. And the poorest families with the biggest problems were taken from the old slums and grouped together. By the late 1930s people claimed that a walk through Blackhill was more dangerous than a walk through parts of the Gorbals.

Privately built bungalows became very popular in the 1930s. This 1933 architect's drawing shows a typical example in Newton Mearns.

The growth of council housing in the 1930s also left council tenants without much say in things. Councillors could decide who should get a house, when they should get it and where it should be, how it should be looked after, whether pets could be kept in it, and even what colour the front door should be painted. They also had power to decide what land to buy and what building contracts to award, and with so much money at stake corruption became more common.

So by the late 1930s Scottish housing was still bad. A survey in 1936 found that almost a half of all Scottish houses were inadequate. Of course the depressed inter-war years were not the ideal time to wrestle with one of the country's biggest problems. Even so, Scotland's houses by the late 1930s were certainly not 'fit for heroes'. Instead, people joked bitterly that you had to be a hero to live in most of them.

Council housing: *Left* Knightswood, 1920s spacious housing and well-kept gardens *Right* Blackhill, 1930s closely packed tenements and wasteland

An ideal kitchen of 1936. For most people, the reality was very different.

Between the wars, it was normal for Scottish women to give up their jobs when they got married. Only about one married woman in twenty went out to work in the 1920s. Instead, they stayed at home and ran the house.

Being a housewife was very hard work, because there were hardly any machines to help: washing machines, dryers, vacuum cleaners, central heating, were all either in the future or were too expensive for most people. So the housewife's job was a never-ending battle against dirt. At the centre of many houses was the kitchen range, a coal-burning monster of steel and iron. It had to be fired up with paper and wood, ashes had to be cleared from it, the iron parts had to be 'blackleaded' and the steel parts rubbed with emery paper. All the cooking had to be done on the range, and water for washing and baths had to be heated on it.

Laundry demanded even more time and effort. Clothes and sheets had to be boiled in tubs, scrubbed and rinsed, wrung out, hung out, taken down and ironed with a 'flat-iron' that had to be kept hot on the range. It was hard and time-consuming work that soon led to raw fingers and tired bodies.

In tenements most of the laundry had to be done in wash-houses, and Molly Weir remembers what a big part of life the wash-houses were in inter-war Glasgow:

'The wash-house was in the back-court, and each one served the twelve families in each tenement close, so a strict rota system operated for all the days of the week. As nobody wanted to wash at the weekends, each person's turn came round every twelve days. Domestic circumstances often led to the mothers swopping days with each other, and that was where the trouble started. If Mrs Brown swopped Tuesday for Thursday, then the woman who was entitled to the key after Mrs Brown had to be alerted, so *she* would know from whom to expect the key. . . . With the meagre wardrobes we all possessed it must have been a nightmare trying to keep families in clean and dry clothes for twelve days between washing days, so an earlier washday was a blessing, and a wet day a tragedy.'

The Birth of Radio

In 1923 a company called the British Broadcasting Company, or BBC, began broadcasting from eight main stations across Britain: five in England, one in Wales, and Glasgow and Aberdeen. Radio had come to Scotland.

At first, people thought of the radio as a toy. Then in 1924 the BBC broadcast a speech by the King. Hardly anyone had heard King George the Fifth's voice before this broadcast; suddenly he was speaking to people in their living rooms, and it started to become clear that this was no toy, but one of the most powerful forms of communication ever invented. The government became even more aware of the power of the radio during the 1926 General Strike. And so in 1926 the government changed the BBC from a private company into a public 'corporation'. From now on, the Prime Minister would appoint a board of governors to keep an eye on things.

By 1933, over 40 per cent of all homes in Scotland had a radio set, and by the late 1930s the majority of homes had one. Reception had improved, and the sets were better. People no longer had to put on earphones to listen. A survey at the time found that the set was often switched on in the morning and left on all day. The radio had become a constant background to home life.

In these early years of broadcasting, the Director General or head of the BBC was a Scottish engineer called John Reith. His strong views and powerful position made him into a man of great influence on British society this century. He had been born in an Aberdeen manse in 1889. He was an impressive, perhaps frightening man to look at, because he was six foot six inches tall, and had a scar across one cheek from a bullet wound received during the Great War.

Reith's view was that the radio should be used to 'improve' people, to broadcast 'all that was best in every department of human knowledge, endeavour, and achievement.' If it also entertained, then that was fine, but entertainment was not really an objective. 'I do not pretend to give the public what it wants', said Reith.

Reith made sure that all the announcers spoke in the same plummy accent that came to be known as BBC English. Empire was pronounced 'Empah', Yorkshire 'Yawksha', and forty-thirty in a tennis match became 'fotty-thetty'. Announcers had to wear dinner jackets when broadcasting, even though the audience could not see them! People were soon accusing Reith of being a 'cultural dictator', a 'Presbyterian prince', a 'Calvinist Czar'.

Despite these criticisms, there were many good things about the BBC that Reith created. It wasn't the slave either of government or big business. It did raise standards in lots of areas, like classical music. And before long it did broadcast sports events and dance music.

But Reith's BBC was very centralised. It was based in London, and the programmes made in London were broadcast across Britain from John O'Groats to Land's End. The BBC's Scottish stations could make their own programmes, but the results tended to be traditional, sentimental, and parochial. So mostly the Scottish stations just relayed programmes from London.

The *Radio Times*. Wireless programmes for Wednesday 24th October 1923.

Sir John Reith in 1935

— RADIO TIMES —

WIRELESS PROGRAMME

.15.—GLASGOW NEWS AND WEATHER FORECAST. SPECIAL ANNOUNCE-MENTS.
).25.—CLOSE DOWN.
ANNOUNCER: A. H. SWINTON PATER-SON.

WEDNESDAY.

3.30—AN HOUR OF MELODY BY THE WIRELESS TRIO.
5.0—5.30.—A TALK TO WOMEN : (a) " Symbols in Japanese Art," Part II. by Mr. C. Pollard Crowther; (b) Beauty Culture by Madame Nesti.
5.30.—THE CHILDREN'S CORNER : (a) " A Japanese Fairy Story," by Uncle C. Pollard Crowther ; (b) " Jack Hardy," Chap. 6, Part II. by Herbert Strang; (c) Competition.
6.0.—SPECIAL WEATHER REPORT FOR FARMERS.
6.15.—BOYS' BRIGADE BULLETIN.
7.0.—THE FIRST GENERAL NEWS BULLETIN BROADCAST FROM LONDON.
7.10.—DR. FRIDTJOF NANSEN, G.C.V.O., the famous Arctic Explorer, will talk on "The Plight of Europe." *S.B. from London.*
7.25.—GLASGOW NEWS AND WEATHER

7.30.—CLASSICAL NIGHT OF THE WIRE-LESS ORCHESTRA. A Night with French Composers. ORCHESTRA : Overture, " Zampa " (*Louis Herold*, born Paris, 1791). MR. PHILLIP MELSOM, Tenor : Will lecture on " Music of the Period 1225—1558," with musical illustrations by the lecturer. MISS CATHIE MAWER, Soprano. OR-CHESTRA : 1st Arabesque (*Claude Debussy*). MR. T. RIDDEL BRECHIN, Bass. ORCHESTRA : Selection, " Samson and Delilah " (*Saint-Saëns*). MISS CATHIE MAWER, Soprano. ORCHESTRA : Suite, " Le Roi S'Amuse " (*Clement Delibes*). MR. T. RIDDEL BRECHIN, Bass.
9.0.—CLOSE DOWN.
9.30.—SECOND GENERAL NEWS BULLE TIN BROADCAST FROM LONDON, followed by GLASGOW NEWS AND WEATHER REPORT.
9.45.—MISS CATHIE MAWER, Soprano. ORCHESTRA : Selection, " Carmen " (*G. Bizet*). MR. T. RIDDEL BRECHIN, Bass : " When the Kye Come Home" (Traditional); " The Trumpeter " (*J. A. Dix*). ORCHESTRA.
10.30.—SPECIAL ANNOUNCEMENTS.
10.35—CLOSE DOWN.
ANNOUNCER : H. A. CARRUTHERS.

THURSDAY.

Going Out

All the new eating and drinking places of the thirties liked to follow the latest styles in design and materials. The most popular style was 'Thirties Moderne'. The Moderne style used new materials like aluminium and chromium-plated metal, glass bricks, a type of coloured sheet-glass called vitrolite, and neon lighting. The designers liked to use zigzag and chevron shapes, and went in for 'streamlining'. After the sensational discovery of the tomb of Tutankhamun in 1922, Egyptian shapes and designs became a very popular part of the Moderne style. These designs and materials could be seen all over Scotland in the 1930s, in cafe counters, chip shop signs, snack bar lights, and tearoom windows and cinemas.

Top Milk Bar in Central Station, Glasgow in 1936   *Above* The Café Moderne, Pollokshaws Road, Glasgow in 1940

For many Scottish adults wanting a night out between the wars, the pub was still the first port of call. There were still plenty of 'spit and sawdust' pubs, full of men standing by the counter and concentrating on drinking. But during the inter-war period there was a trend towards cocktail bars and lounge bars. These were clean and comfortable, with seats and tables and modern lighting. Many of them had staff who wore uniform jackets with white shirts and bow ties. For the first time women started going to these new bars.

But drinking became much less popular between the wars. The government had raised taxes on alcohol.

It had also decided during the Great War to limit the length of time that pubs could stay open, because it was worried about drunkenness interfering with the war effort. So by the 1930s the amount of alcohol drunk in Scotland was only about a quarter of what it had been at the beginning of the century.

Instead of going to pubs, more people went to cafes, which had a hey-day between the wars in Scotland. These were often run by Italians, and had continental names like the Cafe D'Ore, and the Cafe del Rio. Another thirties fad was for snack bars, milk bars, and fast service eating places.

Cinemas had become very popular in Scotland during the 1920s. Glasgow especially was movie-mad. It had 127 cinemas showing silent movies in 1929, more for its size than any other city outside America. One of them was the gigantic Green's Playhouse, which could seat 4400 people and was the largest cinema in Europe. Then in 1929 the 'talkies' arrived, and so during the 1930s the cinema became even more popular.

Scores of new cinemas were opened in Scotland during the 1930s. A lot of them were 'super cinemas', with cafes, milk bars, and restaurants. They were very stylish and Moderne, with lots of neon, streamlining, and even palm courts and fountains in the foyer. No wonder people called them 'picture palaces' or the 'pleasure dome'.

By 1937 Glasgow's cinemas had seats for over 130,000 people. But there was quite a choice of cinemas in almost every town.

The only place that could compete with the cinema for young Scottish people between the wars was the dance-hall. Scotland went 'dance-mad' in the 1920s, as popular new dances swept across the country from Europe and America. The Charleston, the tango and the foxtrot spread like wildfire, (thanks in large part to the radio and cinema) and dance-halls, or 'Palais de danse', could be found in every town, just like the cinema.

John Mathison grew up in Kirkcaldy and remembers all the cinemas and dance-halls in the town during the 1930s:

'You had what was known as the Opera House, the Rialto, the Palace, you had a flea-pit . . . . called the Palladium, you had the Carlton, half-way down St Clair Street, you had the Rio, and you had another one along the links, all these cinemas in Kirkcaldy. And for the average citizen, especially for the young people, you went to the cinema twice a week.

'We didn't have the discos you have today, but there were a large number of dance-halls, small intermediate and large. There was a small dance-hall known as Curry's Dancing, and young people went there on a Thursday or a Saturday between five and seven, to learn to dance; this was known as Curry's Jumpers. And once you got a wee bit experience at Curry's Jumpers you could go down to the major dance-halls in the town. And of the major dance-halls there was the Masonic Dancing, nothing to do with the Freemasonry but just the hall was there. There was another hall called the Burma which held about 200 people, another one above Burton's the Tailors called the Plaza, and along at the beginning of Kirkcaldy, in a place called Olympia Arcade, there was a huge, huge dance-hall, and also to the left of that was a small dance-hall called the Labour Club, plus another one which was in Hunter Street. So, all these things prospered every Saturday night, every one of these dance-halls I've talked about were packed.'

Crowds queueing outside the Coliseum Picture House, Glasgow to see Charlie Chaplin in the film *City Lights*. The photograph was probably taken soon after the film was released, in 1931.

Gangland

Gangs were nothing new in Glasgow. There had been the Penny Mob in the 1890s, the San Toy Boys in the 1900s, the Redskins and Kelly Boys in the 1910s. But in the inter-war years there was a lot more concern about them. The Billy Boys, the Sally Boys, the Norman Conks, the Baltic Fleet and other gangs fought mainly amongst themselves, but they were giving the city a bad name. And other Scottish towns and cities seemed to be copying Glasgow's gangs. By the 1930s the amount of violent crime in Scotland was much higher – perhaps six times higher – than in England. So when Percy Sillitoe was made Glasgow's Chief Constable in 1933, he had plenty of work to do.

Sillitoe waged war on the razor gangs. But to do this he had to reform the police, who had become old-fashioned and ineffective. He introduced patrol-cars with radios, and had Tardis-like police boxes built all over the city. He changed the uniform too, giving the police the flat caps with a chequered band round them. Soon his reforms had been copied by other police forces in Scotland. And by the Second World War, the gang problem had faded away, at least for the time being.

In 1935 two journalists called A. McArthur and H. Kingsley Long wrote a novel called *No Mean City*, about Glasgow's gangs. In this scene, Peter and Isobel are dancing in a hall on the Paisley Road, when they are surrounded by three young men from the Plantation district of Glasgow. They have recognised Peter as the brother of Johnnie Stark, the 'Razor King' who had given them a beating a few weeks earlier:

'. . . Peter pushed Isobel away from him with his free hand and side-stepped towards the wall. But his enemies anticipated him. For a moment his heart sank and then his eyes sparkled with a fighting glint. He did not wait to be attacked: he leaped at his nearest assailant, the tall one with the bottle in his hand, feinted and drove home a smashing left to the ear. The big fellow staggered and swore, but one of his companions struck at Peter from behind, a blow that would have felled him had the bottle fallen full upon his unprotected skull instead of glancing off it. Peter reeled, and Isobel, screaming, ran to catch him. In the same instant the third of the Plantation lads drew his bottle of beer and brought it down savagely on Peter's head. It broke with a loud report. Blood streamed down Peter's forehead and he sagged at the knees.

"That's wan for Razor King!" his opponent shouted. "Tell him Cameron did that te ye! Cameron frae the Toll . . ."'

McArthur and Long called their novel *No Mean City*. It wasn't very good or well written, but it had a huge impact. Its image of Glasgow, as a violent place full of gangs, has lasted a very long time.

Above Chief Constable Percy Sillitoe on parade in 1936. *Below* Spicy newspaper story about gang warfare in Glasgow in 1929

EWS: GLASGOW, FRIDAY, MAY 10, 1929.

GLASGOW GANGSTERS.

Youthful Hooligans Terrorise Small Shopkeepers.

BID TO RIVAL CHICAGO.

GIRL MEMBERS LEAD TO MANY DISPUTES

A special investigation into the activities of the Glasgow gangs was conducted by a representative of The Evening News. The inquiry revealed that these gangs constitute a serious menace to the community.

Their activities are not confined to one city area, but they are specially and notoriously active in Bridgeton and in Govan. The "Nudie Boys" of Bridgeton almost rival the gangsters of Chicago in their threats to the safety of the citizens.

BOTTLES BETTER THAN RAZORS.

The blackmailing activities of some of the Glasgow gangs were revealed to an Evening News representative who carried out an investigation in the areas principally affected. They terrorise the whole community, and particularly the small-shopkeeping class, in order that they may make an easy livelihood without doing any work themselves.

Most of the members of such gangs are unemployed or unemployable youths between 17 and 22. The leader is generally a few years older than his followers, and is chosen principally for his weight and fighting ability. A system of transfers (similar to that which obtains in the football world) is in operation, and when two rival gangs are about to stage a battle good fighters are transferred from one gang to another. Heavy fees are reported to be paid, and as much as £20 has been paid for a single "transfer."

GIRLS OR "MOLLS."

A girl is known to the gangsters as a "Moll." Each gang has a number of such girls attached to it and over these

to deal with these gangs is that a rival gangster never gives the members of an opposing gang away. There is honour among gangsters. One member of a gang who did turn on his erstwhile companions not so long ago went soon after to hospital—as the result of an "accident"—and he is still there. His former colleagues seized him, broke his ribs, and left him lying on the street unconscious.

THE LEADING GANG.

The leading and by far the worst gang is that which operates in Bridgeton under the somewhat inexplicable title of "The Nudie Boys." Other well-known gangs are the "Pikers," and the "Billy Boys." A good fighter (a man who carries a big transfer fee) is one who can "gouge," and who is an expert bottle-thrower. "Gouging" is the most fiendish activity of the gangs. It is an operation whereby one damages an opponent's eye by using the pressure of the forefinger and the thumb.

A bottle-thrower is a particularly useful member of a gang. He throws a bottle in order to strike, and the experts can use two bottles at a time. A

76

Schools

In 1872 the government had separated school and church and set up a national educational system. But the Scottish Catholics had refused to have anything to do with the new system. Instead, they had tried to set up their own school system, where the Catholic Church would still have a say in what was taught.

It didn't take long for differences to appear: the national system was supported by tax-payers' money, while the Catholic schools got no public support. By the early twentieth century the standards of Catholic schools had fallen behind. This created a danger that Scotland's Catholics might become a permanently deprived minority.

And so in 1918 a new system was created. The Catholic schools became part of the national system, and henceforth would get the same support and meet the same teaching standards. But at the same time they were allowed to continue as separate Catholic schools, with the church involved in their religious education.

This was an unusual arrangement. At the time, some people became very worked up about it, and complained of 'Rome on the Rates'. But the Labour Party supported separate Catholic schools in return for Catholic votes, and the system survived these criticisms.

The bad side of the new school system of 1918 was that the Catholic-Protestant division became part of Scottish life from an early age. But the good side was that the system kept the same school standards for Protestants and Catholics.

Scottish education had other big problems between the wars, and many of them got worse rather than better. Partly it was a matter of money. Teachers had to devote too much time to protecting their wages or their jobs. And the school leaving age stayed at 14 although the plan in 1918 had been to raise it to 15.

But money wasn't the only problem. By 1923 the secondary schools had been divided into 'junior secondary' and 'senior secondary' schools. Almost everyone went to a junior secondary for three years and left with no qualifications. A very small minority went to senior secondaries. The theory was that only a few children were 'academic' and would benefit from a better education. But in practice there was no way of telling at the age of eleven or twelve if someone was 'academic' or not. All that happened was that the middle class children went to senior secondaries, the working class to junior secondaries, and so most of the country's talent was ignored.

Ramsay MacDonald, the Prime Minister in 1924 and from 1929 to 1935, was a harsh critic of Scotland's new school system. He argued that it had '. . . nothing to do with the improvement of national education'; instead, '. . . its effect was to form a new series of classes and sub-classes, of servants and masters, of subordinates and superiors, determined by the schools through which they had gone.'

The results of the school system could be seen very clearly in the universities. Between 1926 and 1935, one person in every twenty born in the highest social class went to university, but only one in every five hundred and fifty born in the lowest social class.

People still liked to think that Scottish education was amongst the best anywhere. But Scotland had fallen behind many other countries. There were hardly any nursery schools. Technical subjects were ignored or sneered at by secondary schools. There were very few technical colleges, and hardly any day release courses or vocational training schemes. Money was one of the problems in all these things, but an even bigger problem was the view that, when it came to education, Scotland had nothing to learn from anyone else.

Work to do . . .

1 Study the two photographs of the Knightswood and Blackhill housing schemes. Describe the differences you can see between the two schemes. Then read about them again, and try to explain why they are different.

2 When did the BBC begin broadcasting? Who was John Reith and what did he have to do with the BBC? Why did some people call him a 'cultural dictator'? Do you think that he deserved their nicknames? Why, or why not?

3 Look again at the extract from the *Radio Times* for Wednesday the 24th of October 1923. What do you think of the 'wireless programmes' broadcast that day? Try to get hold of an up-to-date *Radio Times* and look at the programme for Wednesday on Radio 4. What changes have been made since 1923?

4 Why did people drink less alcohol between the wars? By how much did drinking go down between the beginning of the century and the 1930s? Where did many people go instead of the pub?

5 Who was Sir Percy Sillitoe? What big problem did he have to deal with? How did he tackle it?

6 In what ways did Scotland's schools change between the wars? What do you think was good or bad about these changes? What changes would you have made to improve things?

A Scottish Renaissance?

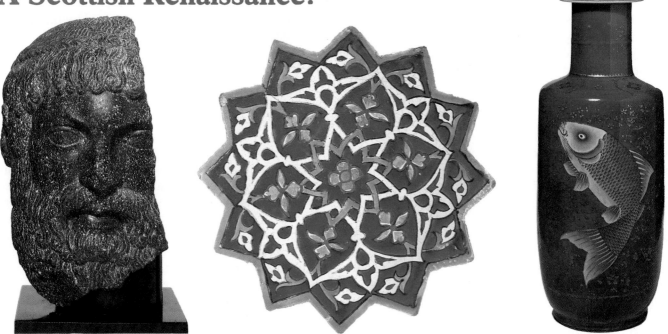

A few items collected by Burrell: *Left* A Roman sculpture of Poseidon or Zeus; *Middle* A Persian star tile; *Right* A Chinese vase decorated with a carp; *Below* A German tapestry fragment showing birds and monsters.

When the war finished and Depression settled over Scotland, the country's artists found it hard to sell their work. When the painter F.C.B. Cadell wrote to the shipping magnate Ian Harrison in 1931, he had a sad story for his friend and supporter: 'Shipping certainly sounds depressing! But everything appears to be in a hopeless state and I have never known such depression in my trade as exists at present. I sell my things now at a quarter of what I got for them some years ago, and I furthermore sell *very* much fewer.'

But there were lots of bargains for anyone with money to spend. William Burrell was in this position. Burrell had sold his fleet of ships just after the Great War had begun, when Britain was desperate for ships and he had been able to ask very high prices. He had been going to auctions and art dealers for years, but now he had the time and money to buy on a grand scale.

Soon Burrell was buying all over the world. He was interested in much more than paintings: he bought sculptures, tapestries, porcelain, metalwork and even stone arches, windows and doorways from old churches. He was interested in works of art from many countries and many periods, from ancient China to modern France. Between 1914 and his death in 1958, Burrell spent on average £20,000 each year on his art collection. Later he would be nicknamed the 'Millionaire Magpie', but he had good advisers, always drove a hard bargain, and was seldom diddled.

Soon Burrell was faced with the problem of finding space for his collection. His home in the West End of Glasgow was bursting at the seams, and so he bought a castle in Berwickshire. It gave him much more space,

but even so it too was soon bulging. The famous art historian Kenneth Clark remembered once visiting Burrell: 'When we first entered our bedroom . . . I said "That's a fine rug, Sir William". "Aye but you'll find a better one underneath." There was, and I said so. "Aye, but the one under that there's a better one still." and so forth for five deep!'

In 1943 Burrell decided to make firm plans for the future of his collection. After much thought, he decided to leave most of it to the city of Glasgow, the place from where he had made his fortune. But finding a permanent home for it in Glasgow was to be another story.

Hugh MacDiarmid

A portrait of Hugh MacDiarmid in 1962

MacDiarmid's most famous poem is called 'A Drunk Man Looks at the Thistle'. In parts of it, MacDiarmid talks about himself:

'I'll hae nae hauf-way hoose, but aye be whaur
Extremes meet – it's the only way I ken
To dodge the curst conceit o' bein' richt
That damns the vast majority o' men.

I'll bury nae heid like an ostrich's
Nor yet believe my een and naething else.
My senses may advise me, but I'll be
Mysel' ae maitter what they tell's . . .'

'Later in the poem, he writes about Scotland:

'O Scotland is
The barren fig
Up, carles, up
and roon it jig.

Auld Moses took
A dry stick and
Instantly it
Floo'ered in his hand.

Pu' Scotland up,
and wha can say
it winna bud
And blossom tae.'

In these two extracts, MacDiarmid uses words like 'een' for 'eyes' and 'whaur' for 'where', but in other poems he sometimes used old Scots words that no-one ever speaks or understands. In fact he kept a Scots dictionary by his desk, and often browsed through it looking for words he could use.

The 1920s and 1930s saw a flood of good work by Scotland's novelists, poets, dramatists, and essayists. Some people started talking about a 'Scottish Renaissance'. And no-one wrote or talked more about it than Christopher Murray Grieve, who was born in Langholm in the Borders in 1892. Grieve wrote under various different names during his life, (his *noms de plume* included Arthur Leslie, Gilliechrood Mac a'Ghreidhir, and even Isobel Guthrie!), but he has become best known as Hugh MacDiarmid.

MacDiarmid thought that Scotland had made a terrible mistake in forming a union with England in 1707. He was strongly anti-English, and raged against Scots who favoured all things English, calling them a ' . . . whole gang of high mucky-mucks, famous fatheads . . . touts and toadies and lickspittles . . . .' His life became a campaign to create a Scotland that was independent. Part of the campaign was political. He wrote endless numbers of pamphlets, ranted from soapboxes, and helped to found the National Party of Scotland in 1928. The other part of the campaign was literary. He was a poet, and wanted to revive the Scots language by showing in his poetry how powerful and beautiful it could be.

MacDiarmid spent his whole life in the middle of arguments. He said rude things about his home town, and once asked for the inscription on his tombstone to be 'A disgrace to the community'. His political views were always starting arguments, and in the space of a few years he was thrown out of the Scottish National Party for being a Communist, then thrown out of the Communist Party for being a Nationalist.

But the fiercest arguments of all have been over his poetry. Many people have described him as a genius, while others have called him 'demented' or a 'madman'. Although he died in 1978 the arguments are bound to go on. Perhaps the best epitaph to MacDiarmid was written by himself, when he stated that 'my job, as I see it, has never been to lay a tit's egg, but to erupt like a volcano, emitting not only flame, but a lot of rubbish.'

John Grierson: Film Maker

John Grierson (on the right) directs during the filming of *Drifters*.

By the 1920s and 1930s the way to reach really big audiences was through the new mass media of radio and cinema. And television lay just a few years ahead.

Several Scots sensed the great power of these new media. We have already met John Reith, who became head of the BBC. Another important figure was John Grierson, who was born at Deanston near Stirling in 1898. After the Great War, Grierson got a grant of money to go to America and continue his studies. He went to Chicago.

America was the home of the movie industry, and soon Grierson was fascinated by movies. They provided mass entertainment, but Grierson began to see that they could do much more than that. Cities like Chicago were full of immigrants who came from all over the world, speaking every language but English. The movies brought them together, and helped them to speak English and feel American.

Grierson travelled all over America, from New York to Hollywood, speaking to film-makers and finding out as much as he could. He also studied carefully the work of the leading Russian film-makers. He decided that film was the best way – perhaps the only way – of getting ordinary people to understand their own society and the problems facing it.

The type of film Grierson had in mind was the 'documentary'. Documentaries were not new but Grierson had some new ideas about them. He thought they should explain, but also that they should inspire. 'I look on cinema as a pulpit', he said.

And he wanted to make documentaries in which ordinary people spoke about their own lives: he called it the 'drama of the doorstep'.

In 1927 Grierson returned to Britain, and was given some money to make a documentary about the herring industry. He set off for the north-east of Scotland with a small crew and started filming.

By 1929 the film was ready. It was a 50-minute silent film called *Drifters*. It showed the daily work of the fishermen, the ports, the boats and the fish-markets. Working men were normally ignored or shown as comical idiots in British films of that time; Grierson put them at the centre of *Drifters* and showed them as heroes.

A still from *Seawards the Great Ships*, filmed in the Clydeside shipyards in 1958

The film caused a sensation. Film-makers flocked to him to follow his example. He was given more money. And so a string of films followed *Drifters*, all made under Grierson's supervision. *Housing Problems*, made in 1935, was a shocking documentary that exposed dreadful rat-infested and damp slums, and let people talk directly to the camera about the way they were forced to live. Soon afterwards came *Night Mail*, a film about the mail-train rushing northwards to Glasgow through a dark Britain. It was real, but it was also wonderfully vivid and imaginative. It was the 'poetry of reality'.

By the late 1930s Grierson had become quite a famous figure in world cinema. Many countries wanted his services. In 1938 he was invited to Canada, and there he set up a National Film Board. It has kept Canada in the front rank of documentary film-making ever since. Later, he had a big influence on the Film Boards of Australia, New Zealand, South Africa and India.

But what of Scotland? Grierson did come back in 1958 to start a series for Scottish Television called *This Wonderful World*. It was popular, and ran weekly for about ten years. It was a programme of film clips from documentaries, but they were made in other countries, not in Scotland. He did supervise one outstanding documentary about the Clyde shipyards called *Seawards the Great Ships*, but it was made by an American. Perhaps the problem was lack of money, for film-making is a frighteningly expensive business. But maybe he put his finger on another problem when he made this comment a few years before his death in 1972: 'Well, the Scots', he said, 'I know them well as people who would not recognise a prophet in their own country. It happens elsewhere too, but nowhere to such a degree as in my own home country.'

Work to do . . .

1 Find out what 'nom de plume' means. What was Christopher Grieve's most famous nom de plume?
2 Read the two extracts from 'A Drunk Man Looks at the Thistle' (read them aloud if possible). Then write ten lines saying what you liked or did not like about them.
3 John Grierson is most famous for 'documentary' films. How would you describe the difference between documentary films and other films? Make a list of documentary films you can remember seeing.

The Highlands between the Wars

A Cruel Homecoming

Scotland's Highlands and Islands had lost a higher proportion of men during the Great War than almost any part of Britain. So when men began to return home from the Highland regiments and the Royal Navy in the winter of 1918, they were met with a feeling of relief rather than celebration. What was there to celebrate, when as many as one in six of all the recruits had been killed?

The cruellest blow of all fell on the people of Lewis. On December 31st 1918 they were getting ready to give 500 servicemen a welcome home. The men were at Kyle of Lochalsh, waiting to sail across to Stornoway on the last stage of their long journey home. They couldn't all get onto the mailboat *Sheila*, so the navy produced a naval yacht, the *Iolaire*, to help out. About 260 of the men, all naval ratings, boarded the *Iolaire*, and at 7.30 pm, it set sail for Stornoway. By midnight they were in the middle of the Minch, and although a storm was rising from the south they yelled and shouted with joy. The old year, the war, could be left behind as the calendar moved on.

Soon they were within sight of the Arnish light at the entrance to Stornoway harbour, and although they couldn't see the quayside a mile away through the stormy darkness, they knew that a huge crowd would be there to welcome them. No doubt the men began to cram along the railings of the ship.

Suddenly, the *Iolaire* was aground. Somehow it had over-run its course and smashed into the wicked rock called the Beast of Holm that guards the eastern side of the harbour entrance. It hit the rock with tremendous force, swung round and lurched over.

Sixty men were thrown into the sea by the force of the impact, or washed overboard by the waves that were now crashing over the *Iolaire*. All of them drowned. Yet the stern of the ship had come to rest only about 20 feet from dry land. So many men were tempted to make a jump for safety. Most of them jumped instead to their death in the wild black water and the jagged rocks. 285 men including the crew had left Kyle of Lochalsh; 206 of them died that stormy night.

The wives and children, parents and neighbours, friends and lovers that had gathered by the quayside couldn't see what had happened. They crowded together in happy anticipation while the returning men were drowned or dashed to pieces a mile away. They began to realise that a disaster had happened only when the first survivors staggered into the town. And only when the bodies were washed ashore did many of the islanders discover that the man whose homecoming they were awaiting had survived the Great War, only to die on his native shore a stone's throw from home. Peacetime in the Highlands had begun ominously.

A memorial to those who died in the *Iolaire* disaster stands at the entrance to Stornoway harbour.

Bad Times for Fishing

With the war over, most people thought that a bright future was in store for fishing. All the wartime restrictions would be swept away, and fishing grounds that had been closed would be reopened.

In fact, things could hardly have turned out more badly. By 1919 the hundreds of fishing boats that had been working for the Royal Navy were free again to go fishing. It meant that there were far more boats chasing the same number of fish, and many boats could not make enough money to stay in business. On top of that, it was far more difficult to sell fish. Before the war, most of the herring that were caught were sold to Germany and Russia. But Germany was in chaos after the war, and the Russian Revolution had put a stop to Scottish exports there. And as the years passed it became obvious that these old markets had gone for good. At home, too, people were eating a lot less fish. There were a lot of reasons for this. People began to dislike the smell of herring cooking in small kitchens. Children didn't like all the little bones in it. It came to be thought of as the 'poor man's fish'.

And so the inter-war years were black for the fishermen and for the towns and villages that depended on the sea's harvest. Boats rotted and rusted, weeds grew on the quaysides, and the thick forests of masts that had once filled the fishing ports became a fading memory of better days.

Land Raids

Many men returning from the war had high hopes of getting some crofting land. Their hopes had been raised during the war by the government, which had made lavish promises about land in the future as a way of encouraging recruitment.

> The hopes of the returning men were shared by many other Highlanders. On Lewis in 1917, for example, one speaker told a meeting at Barvas:
>
> 'What are we going to do with our soldiers and sailors? We must look after the men who have fought for us. We must see that they get the land. (loud applause) It is morally theirs. Is there a landlord in the British Empire who would grudge them the soil which they so bravely defended from the savage and brutal Huns?'

The government's promises were not all empty. In 1912, it had set up a Board of Agriculture to acquire estates or large farms and convert them into small-holdings for crofters.

But the Board had been slow and timid in acquiring land. By the end of the Great War it only had about eighty thousand hectares to give out, whereas it needed over six times that amount to satisfy everyone that had applied.

THE LEWIS PROBLEM.

CAN A SOLUTION BE FOUND?

LORD ADVOCATE'S VISIT TO ISLAND.

Mr M. C. Macaulay, secretary of the Demobilised Soldiers' and Sailors' Association, said they all knew they had gathered that day to protest against the action of the raiders at Coll and Gress. (Applause and a Voice—"Against them we're here"). They had illegally seized land which was required in connection with Lord Leverhulme's development schemes, and they had

BROUGHT THE SCHEMES TO A STANDSTILL.

Before the war the only thing a young Lewisman had to look forward to was the land and the fishing, but as their Chairman had told them things had entirely changed since the island was bought by Lord Leverhulme. (Applause). Everyone in his hearing knew that a croft in Lewis could not now support any man, and as a proof of that they could take the case of the raiders themselves who, notwithstanding all the support they had received from the Bolshevik element in Glasgow and elsewhere, had to leave the land and seek a living at the East Coast and English fishings. (Applause). Did that point to the possibility of a croft in Lewis being sufficient to keep a man or that they should go down on their hands and knees to ask for crofts? ("No," and applause). They wanted work, not crofts. They had had enough of crofts. (Loud applause). He was a crofter's son, born and bred at Shader, Point, and he knew what life on a croft was. The conditions under which they were compelled to live as regards housing and everything else were such that he would be ashamed to speak of them. They were certainly not conditions

"FIT FOR HEROES TO LIVE IN."
(A Voice—"The cause of it?") The cause of it was the action of 26 or 27 would-be ex-Service men—(Voices, "Would-be, would-be," and applause). He had nothing to say against any man because he had not been in France, Mesopotamia, the Dardanelles or Salonica, or against the man who had volunteered and had been sent home before the war was over, but he said this without fear of contradiction that of the men who at Coll and Gress had been making capital out of the word "ex-Service," there were only about four who had heard a gun fired since the big gun was removed from the Battery at Stornoway, and (Voices, "Too true," "Rub it in, Murdo," and loud applause). According to the 1911 census the population was 29,604, and out of that no less than 6196 had served in the Army and Navy. Lord Leverhulme had come forward with great schemes that, if they had been allowed to go on, would have raised the whole population of the island to a higher standard of living, by giving work on the Island and obviating the necessity for Lewismen going to Glasgow or the Colonies to earn a living. (Applause). Of the 6000 men who had served, practically all who returned

SAW THE GREAT CHANCE
Lord Leverhulme's schemes offered and they grasped at it. But the so-called ex-Service men who had raided the farms came forward and they said, "There are 27 of us: we'll bring the Island to their knees," and they had done it. (A Voice—"Up till now," and applause). Concluding, he said that while they spoke as they did about the raiders, they had really nothing against the raiders as men; it was their policy they opposed—a policy adopted by them at the instance of, and with the assistance of, Bolshevik elements in the south who had no interest in the Island of Lewis except to make trouble in it. (Loud applause).

Mr J. G. Macaskill, workers' representative on the Labour Exchange, moved the following resolution :—

"That we place our views regarding the Lewis and Harris developments schemes before the Rt Honourable T. B. Morison

Above Newspaper report of a meeting of ex-servicemen in Stornoway in 1920, to discuss the land problem and the landraiding *Below* Emigrants bid farewell to Stornoway from the *Marloch* in 1924.

Men who had applied for land were in no mood to hang about waiting. Nor were they in any mood to go begging for land, especially from absentee owners like Lady Gordon Cathcart, who had owned the Barra Isles for 54 years but had visited them just once. And so men began to help themselves to land. Landraiding returned to the Highlands and Islands.

In 1918 the raids began in Barra, Uist, Tiree, and Sutherland. In 1919 there were more raids, especially at Glendale in South Uist and Kinlochmearig in North Harris. 1920 saw 16 raids. In 1921 raiders from the island of Rona crossed to Raasay where they built houses and began to farm the land.

The raiding would have continued, but by 1922 the cold winds of industrial depression had reached the furthest corners of the Highlands and Islands. Even at the best of times it had been impossible to make a living just from a croft: the crofters had to find work in the towns in winter, or spend part of their time fishing. But by 1922 there were very few jobs to be had in the depressed towns of Scotland, and fishing too was in a bad way. The dream that so many highlanders must have clung to in the trenches, of a peaceful life back home on their own land, had been dashed.

And so thousands of men began to withdraw their applications for land, and applied instead for a passage on the emigrant ships. The sight off Stornoway in April 1923 was typical of the Highlands at that time: the Canadian Pacific liner *Metegama* about to set sail with a full load of emigrants. Almost all the 300 people from Lewis who boarded the *Metegama* were young men, with an average age of 22. They were off to Ontario in Canada, where they had each been offered 40 hectares of land. Another country had held out the opportunity that Scotland had promised but failed to provide.

A Pattern of Islands

Below Lord Leverhulme, who bought Lewis in 1917, had plans to rebuild Stornoway. This drawing shows a towering war memorial on the South Beach Quay, a broad avenue leading to a new town hall and art gallery, and a railway station with lines fanning out across the island. As the modern photograph on the right shows, none of these schemes came to anything.

Almost every Scottish island saw its population fall between the wars. But no two islands were alike. On Orkney, farming brought prosperity. When the writer Edwin Muir reached Orkney during his journey round Scotland in 1933 he found 'hardly a trace of the widespread poverty that one finds both in the big towns and the countryside of middle and southern Scotland'.

Island prosperity was also the aim of the English industrialist Lord Leverhulme. He bought the island of Lewis in 1917 and drew up plans to modernize it. But his plans did not get the backing of all the islanders, and within a few years he had sold up and left.

Iona's fortunes also changed between the wars. A socialist minister called George MacLeod began to rebuild the historic Abbey on Iona, and got backing from the shipping magnate James Lithgow. In time, MacLeod's work would attract many more visitors to the little island.

The Death of St Kilda

In 1930 one island became famous when everyone left – St Kilda.

St Kilda is really a group of islands in the Atlantic Ocean about one hundred and ten miles west of the Scottish mainland. The main island, Hirta, is only one and a half miles long and a little more across.

Life on St Kilda was isolated. The islanders never paid any tax or rates because no-one ever bothered to send them forms. They never cast votes in elections or fought in a war. 'All beyond their little rock home is darkness, doubt and dread', wrote one visitor in 1875.

In the nineteenth century, with the invention of the steamship, St Kilda became a popular trip for tourists. The tourists were the beginning of the end for St Kilda. Their money changed the way of life. Their ideas and influence made the St Kildans aware of the outside world and dissatisfied with their own rocky world. And the tourists left their own deadly souvenir, in the shape of infectious diseases like the common cold. Mainlanders were used to these diseases and had developed a resistance to them, but the islanders were not used to them and had no resistance. They learned to fear the 'boat-cold' which sometimes swept through them after a tourist visit, because it could leave them in bed for weeks, and could even kill them.

The Great War brought the end closer for St Kilda. The Royal Navy decided to put up a signal station, with fifteen men, a wireless, and regular supplies. It gave the St Kildans a taste of the good things in life, especially regular and varied food. When the war finished, quite a few of the younger St Kildans decided to leave the islands for the mainland, and the population fell. By 1923 it was down from around one hundred to seventy-five. In 1926 an epidemic of influenza ran through the islanders. It killed four of them,

and badly dented the spirit of the remainder. By 1928 only 37 St Kildans were left on the island. By 1930 they had given up the struggle, and had no real desire to spend another winter on St Kilda. On the 10th of May that year they drew up a petition to the Secretary of State for Scotland. It began: 'We the undersigned, the natives of St Kilda, hereby respectfully pray and petition H M Government to assist us all to leave the island this year and find homes and occupations for us on the mainland.'

Even while the government fussed about the arrangements, another young islander died of tuberculosis before help could be sent. Finally, on 29th August 1930, the 36 remaining St Kildans boarded HMS *Harebell* and were taken to the mainland.

The Scottish Office had decided that there would be no reporters or photographers or cinema newsreels present when the St Kildans finally left their home. But one journalist called Alasdair Alpin McGregor, who had been sent from London by *The Times* to cover the story, was there almost to the end. 'The loneliest of Britain's island-dwellers' he wrote, 'have resigned their heritage to the ghosts and the sea-birds; and the curtain is rung down on haunted homes and the sagas of the centuries.' Sir Reginald MacLeod of MacLeod, who owned the islands, was less romantic: 'I am sorry to lose a population that has down its generations been tenants of my family for a thousand years. But they themselves have elected to go, and I cannot blame them. The life is one of hardship and inconvenience.'

Since 1956 St Kilda has been owned by the National Trust for Scotland. They have worked to restore and maintain the buildings. And since 1957 Hirta has had new inhabitants: an army team in a radar station that tracks missiles fired from the Uist test-range. So the St Kildans are gone, but St Kilda has not yet been surrendered to the storms and seabirds.

The crumbling Main Street, Village Bay, St Kilda

The Shape of Things to Come?

Argyll Forest Park has been popular for a day out for over 50 years.

The inter-war years saw the beginning of some new activities in the Highlands, activities that would become more important as time went by. Hydro-electric schemes began to change the landscape, flooding the glens beneath reservoirs. The Rannoch scheme began in 1930, the Tummell scheme in Perthshire in 1933.

Even bigger changes to the Highland landscape were begun by the Forestry Commission. It had been set up by the government in 1919, to make sure that in any future blockades Britain would have its own supplies of timber. Soon it was at work, buying up land, draining it and fencing it to keep out the deer, then planting rows upon rows of trees. It built miles of new roads, too, in order to get access to the forests.

At first, the Forestry Commission paid no attention to what anyone else might think of its activities. Its trees marched up the sides of hills in great dark rectangles, looking ugly and unnatural. But by the 1930s it was beginning to make some provision for tourists and visitors. It started to create Scottish Forest Parks, with camp-sites, paths, and picnic areas. The first was the Argyll Forest Park, stretching down the western side of Loch Long almost to the outskirts of Dunoon. It opened in 1935, helping to attract people from nearby Glasgow who wanted to escape from the city for the day.

The Highlands between the wars also became a way of escaping from the dole queues and depression of Scotland's towns and cities. Unemployed people began to go climbing and walking on Scotland's hills. If they could afford to, they took a train or a bus. If not, they hitched a lift, or cycled or walked. They stayed in cheap tents that had appeared as a result of the Everest expeditions of the 1920s, or if they couldn't afford a tent they stayed in old huts or even under boulders.

Eventually, some of them formed clubs and scraped together enough money to buy or build their own hut in some favourite part of the Highlands. Jock Nimlin formed the Ptarmigan Club in 1929, and other famous clubs like the Creag Dhu Club were formed at around the same time. So slowly a new future was appearing for the Highlands, as a huge playground to which people could escape from the towns and cities.

Jock Nimlin remembers going on climbing trips to the Scottish mountains during the 1920s. He had a job, and had to work until 9 pm on a Saturday. As soon as he finished work, he got a late train or bus as close as he could get to the mountains:

'If you were going to Arrochar, for example, you got as far as Balmaha and Loch Lomond and we had an arrangement with the boat hirer there to leave out a boat and two sets of oars and we would board the boat perhaps eight of us, sometimes ten of us, we sometimes had the boat overloaded and off we would go about midnight from Balmaha and we would row fourteen miles up to Tarbet.

Then we would pull the boat ashore, snatch a few hours' sleep under trees until daylight and then we'd have a very early breakfast and walk across to Arrochar and from Arrochar we would climb the Cobbler, Ben Ime, Ben Narnain, any of the mountains in that vicinity, and in the early evening, we would make a point of getting back to the boat, back into the loch again and we had that fourteen miles to row, back to Balmaha. Of course we always tried our best to get the last bus at Balmaha but on one or two occasions we were held up by headwinds and we missed the last bus at Balmaha which meant that we had to walk from Balmaha right back into Glasgow again to start work on the following morning.'

It could all be 'super-strenuous', but there were quite a lot of people like Jock Nimlin.

Work to do . . .

1 Why did many people think that the end of the Great War meant good times ahead for fishing? Describe what in fact happened, and why.
2 Imagine that you are one of the emigrants about to set sail from the Highlands in the 1920s. Write a short story about your reasons for leaving, and the way you feel about the past and the future. (If you think it might help you, study the photograph of emigrants and try to imagine how they felt at the time.)
3 Look closely at the drawing and the photographs of Stornoway, then list any differences you can spot between them.
4 Describe in about ten lines the events that made St Kilda famous between the wars.

Speeding Up

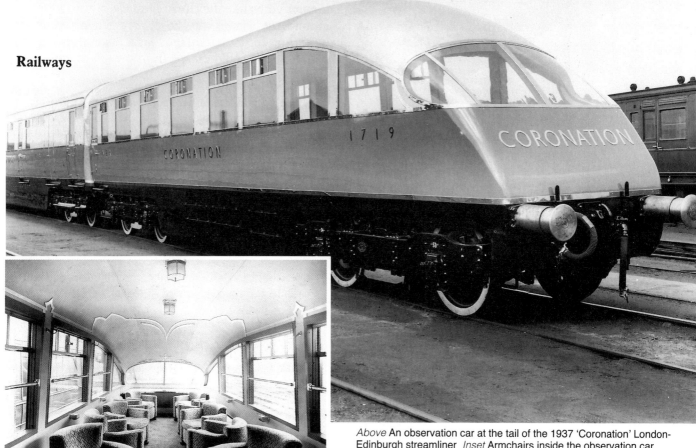

Above An observation car at the tail of the 1937 'Coronation' London-Edinburgh streamliner *Inset* Armchairs inside the observation car

The railways emerged from the Great War in a mess. Some lines, like the Highland line carrying supplies for Scapa Flow, had been used far more heavily than the builders had ever intended. So many railway staff had been in the armed forces that hardly any maintenance or repairs had been done. The railway companies didn't have the money to put things right. They were losing money, and were close to bankruptcy.

Only the government was in a position to sort out the mess, but the Conservatives in Lloyd George's Coalition government didn't like the idea of nationalisation, or the idea of spending public money on reconstruction.

So a new solution was found: the railways were grouped into four private companies. The railways in the east of Scotland became part of the London and North Eastern Railway (LNER), and the railways in the west of Scotland and England were joined to make the London, Midland and Scottish (LMS) railway. The new companies began in 1923.

During the 1920s hardly anything was done to make the railways more modern. The fastest trains from Kings Cross to Edinburgh or Euston to Glasgow took more than eight hours, just as they had in the late nineteenth century. The only new thing was a luggage van attached to LNER trains in 1924 that showed silent feature films! And because of the depression there was a lot less freight to be carried by rail. So railway lines began to close.

The only excitement was when another competition broke out between the London-Scotland expresses. It began in 1928, when the LNER started a new non-stop express between King's Cross and Edinburgh called the *Flying Scotsman*.

The LNER knew that passengers could always be attracted by more space. In 1937 it unveiled its 'secret weapon': high speed trains with specially designed streamlined locomotives and luxury coaches. The train was called the *Coronation*, and by 1938 it had cut the journey time between London and Edinburgh by one quarter, from eight hours to six. It was the 'star turn' of Britain's railways.

Trams and Trolleys

Union Street, Glasgow in April 1939

No-one who used these trams will ever forget the sensation of being on the old Standard Tramcars, as they made their way along the tramlines embedded in the street, their overhead trolleys brushing along the electric cables slung above them. Molly Weir, in a book about growing up in Glasgow between the wars, remembers how the tramcars were once painted different colours on different routes. Then the Corporation decided to use numbers instead, and so queues of people would stand there, trying to decide if it was the right tram for them, while an impatient conductress shouted at them 'Come on, youse. Whit are youse waitin' for? The baund tae play?'

She also remembers how the tram would some-times stop without warning:

'There would be a lurch, and the trolley would come bouncing off the overhead wire in a shower of sparks, and swing wildly back and forth as the car slithered to a halt. This was a nerve-racking experi-ence for the timid, and there would be shouts, "The trolley's off – the trolley's off", and all eyes would fasten anxiously on the conductor as he swung it towards the overhead wire again.

There was no danger, but it made us all uneasy to feel we were sitting there unconnected to that magic overhead wire. If this happened three or four times in the course of a journey, there would be alarmed tut-tutting from the women, and con-temptuous opinions from the men that the driver had "nae idea how to drive a caur". "Aye, he must be new", somebody would murmur, there were plenty of back-seat drivers.'

By the early twentieth century most Scottish towns of any size relied on trams to move people around: amongst them Aberdeen, Ayr, Dundee, Dunfermline, Edinburgh, Glasgow, Greenock and Port Glasgow, Hamilton, Kilmarnock, Motherwell and Wishaw, Musselburgh, Paisley, Perth, and Stirling and Falkirk.

Most of the tramlines had been electrified early in the century. Edinburgh was behind the times: its trams had to reach down under the road and grab hold of moving cables that were driven in an endless loop by stationary steam engines. In 1922, however, the whole system was brought up to date. On the morning of October 22nd, people in Princes Street were amazed to see that overhead electricity cables for the trams had been put up overnight.

Glasgow's trams were widely known as the cheap-est and most efficient in the whole of Britain. The City Corporation had been running the trams since 1894, and in the 1920s it took over the tram systems of towns around Glasgow and ran them all as one big network. By 1923 it was possible to ride from Airdrie to Kil-barchan for less than 1p.

By the Second World War, over 1200 tramcars were at work on the tramlines that criss-crossed the Glasgow area, and people boasted with some truth that there was 'always a tram in sight'.

On the Buses

Alexander's Bus Company made a big impact on the public in 1934 with their 'Bluebird' buses. The design was copied from American buses, and had a 'Bluebird' insignia copied from Imperial Airways. It used fashionable materials like chrome and aluminium that people thought of as modern. It was a 'streamlined', single-decker coach, not an old-fashioned double-decker. And it had pneumatic tyres, and heaters inside.

Top A Bluebird bus owned by W. Alexander and Co. in 1934 *Above* A modern impression of a 1930s bus station

From the early years of the twentieth century a new sight could be seen on the roads of Scotland, that in time would challenge tram and train. This was the motor bus. The very first company was set up in Edinburgh in 1905. It was called the Scottish Motor Traction Company, or S.M.T., and between the wars it became the biggest bus company in Scotland.

The early buses were open to the skies. In fact they were really lorries, and were used as lorries during the week. Then at weekends a few benches were put on the back to make a bus. If it rained, the driver tried to find a bridge to stop under while a hood was put up over the passengers. Some of these early buses ran on gas rather than petrol, and drove along with a huge gas bag billowing above them.

After 1918 there were lots of surplus lorries that had been built for the army. There were also lots of men who had been trained as motor mechanics by the army. So lots of new bus companies were started up. By the mid-1920s there were about 30 bus companies just running between Glasgow and Paisley.

But gradually a few larger bus companies were formed, and took over or put out of business the small companies. One of them was Alexander's of Falkirk. When Walter Alexander started in the business in 1917, he was 15 and the company had six buses.

By 1924 it had grown quickly to 120 buses. As it grew, it started running longer routes: at first around Falkirk, and Denny, but soon to Aberdeen and Inverness. The early journeys could not have been very comfortable, for the buses had solid tyres and the roads were awful. The top speed was about 20 miles per hour in the 1920s.

By the 1930s the roads were getting better, and so were the buses.

Buses were cheaper and more convenient than trains in many country areas, and in smaller towns they forced the trams out of business. But a lot of the traffic on the buses wasn't taken away from the trams or railways: it was new traffic that they had created for themselves. For instance, they started running coach tours around the countryside, which were soon popular amongst tourists and town dwellers alike.

Pioneers of the Air

During the Great War an aircraft industry grew up, and by 1918 Britain's air force had grown into the largest in the world, with over 23,000 aircraft and about 700 aerodromes.

So after the war the 'raw materials' existed to start passenger airlines. Almost immediately two companies started a cross-Channel passenger service. Talk began about a great network of air routes around the world linking the Empire, and a favourite phrase was that Egypt would become the Empire's 'Clapham Junction of the air'.

William Weir, who had been in charge of aircraft production during the last two years of the war, was asked in 1919 to lead an inquiry into the future of civil aviation. His conclusion was that civil aviation had an important future, but that it needed help from the government to get going.

But no help came. British civil aviation got off to a slow start, while the Americans and French raced ahead.

This argument about air travel mattered a lot to Scotland. An air service would have made Scottish business less remote from London and other centres. Inside Scotland, too, there were lots of remote areas where surface travel was difficult and slow, and air travel would be ideal. Finally, there was the beginning of an aircraft building industry in Scotland, just the sort of skilled light engineering with good future prospects that Scotland was crying out for. But it was not until the 1930s that civil aviation reached Scotland. That it did was due to the efforts of pioneering individuals.

Scotland Learns to Fly

Flying circuses were popular in the 1920s. They gave short flights to people who had never flown before. The Americans had invented this, and given it a name: joy-riding. The joy-riding circus, which was a few small two-seat aeroplanes, would arrive at some town, circle around looking for a nice big flat field to land in, then touch down and make a deal with the farmer to use his field for a few days.

These early flyers didn't need to advertise very much. An aeroplane was so unusual in most places that people would drop everything and come running. Even in small towns crowds of two thousand or more might turn up.

In 1931 a man called E. E. Fresson decided to do a long tour through Scotland with a flying circus, going to places that hadn't seen many aircraft before. He visited Denny, Alloa, Kirkintilloch, Kirriemuir, Nairn, Granton, Wick, Kirkwall and other places. Business was very good, but it was hard work: in one day's flying at Renfrew, Fresson did one hundred and fourteen take-offs and landings! And it couldn't last forever. Soon the novelty of aeroplanes would wear off.

Then one day in Wick someone asked him how much it would cost to fly to Kirkwall in Orkney. This wasn't a joy-rider, it was a fare-paying passenger, Fresson's first. And when the journey was over, Fresson realised that a passenger service could be a big success. The usual boat and road journey from Wick to Kirkwall took six hours. If the sea was rough the trip might be impossible. By aeroplane it took 35 minutes, no matter how rough the sea.

A ceremony at Longman Airport marks the start of Britain's first internal airmail service. It linked Inverness and Orkney. E. E. Fresson, who started Highland Airways, is standing to the right of the bald man facing the camera.

AT LAST
SPEEDY & COMFORTABLE
AIR TRAVEL

To the North
of Scotland
and the
Orkney Islands

SANDA

KIRKWALL

THURSO

WICK

City
and
Royal Burgh
of
Kirkwall

SPEND YOUR
HOLIDAYS IN
BEAUTIFUL ORKNEY
SHOOTING·FISHING
GOLF & POINTS OF
HISTORICAL·INTEREST

LOSSIEMOUTH

ELGIN

An Invaluable
Service to the
Business Man

INVERNESS

HIGHLAND AIRWAYS LTD.

He started looking for suitable fields for an air-service from Inverness via Wick to Kirkwall. Then he borrowed some money to buy a plane. On 8th May 1933 the first flight of his new service took off from Inverness with three passengers, and arrived at Orkney one hour and fifteen minutes after leaving. Highland Airways was in business.

Fresson had soon proved that the new air service was convenient and reliable. By May 1934 the General Post Office had allowed Highland Airways to carry the mail between Inverness and Kirkwall. It was Britain's first inland airmail service.

It was obvious, too, that an air service would be ideal for the small islands. By August 1934 North Ronaldsay had an airservice to Kirkwall three days a week. Instead of a boat journey lasting all day, the islanders could take a 15 minute flight, go to the Kirkwall market with their chickens, ducks and eggs, and return the same day.

Ambulance flights were another new service that Highland Airways soon started. Life on small northern islands became a lot easier when people knew that they could be flown in minutes to Balfour Hospital in Kirkwall.

Other pioneers were opening up air services in other parts of Scotland. From Renfrew, William Cumming pushed routes to the western parts of Scotland: to Campbeltown and Islay, Barra, South and North Uist. Fresson joined forces with this outfit in 1935, and they became Scottish Airways. Then the railway companies set up their airline, and by 1936 were flying from Renfrew to Liverpool and Belfast. A few big companies were taking the place of the pioneers.

Passengers on Scotland's first airlines had to share the pioneering spirit. The writer Eric Linklater came from Orkney:

'Once, I remember, I drove to Kirkwall in a great hurry, without having booked a passage, and pleaded with Fresson to take me to Inverness. He said, "I am flying a full load of mail, but if you like to lie on top of the mail bags, you can come." After we had crossed the Pentland firth he turned and shouted, "I hope you won't mind if I go out of my way a bit. I've got very interested in fulmar gulls, and for the last week or two I've been counting their nests". Then, to my horror, he drove his aeroplane along the top edge of the Caithness cliffs, weaving in and out, with his head over his right shoulder and his right hand scribbling notes and details of what he saw.'

Work to do . . .

1 Why were the railways in a mess by 1918? What was done to try to improve things? Were there many improvements during the 1920s or the 1930s?
2 Think about the differences between tramcars and buses, then list some of the good and bad things about each. Do you think it would be a good idea to bring tramcars back to Scotland's streets? Explain your answer.
3 Look at the advertisement for Highland Airways, and make a note of the things it mentions ('speedy and comfortable', 'holidays', etc). Then design your own advert, pretending that it is the 1930s and you are trying to persuade people of the advantages of flying.

Opposite Highland Airways advertise their new services, 1934

The Second World War

The Origins of the Second World War

After 1918 the last thing that most Scots wanted to think about was another war. Had not the Great War been the 'war to end all wars'? And yet by 1939 Britain was once again at war, and once again the main enemy was Germany.

Many of the seeds of the Second World War were sown just after the Great War ended, by the Versailles Treaty of 1919. This was a plan for peace drawn up by the three main victors of the war – America, Britain and France – during a conference at Versailles near Paris. The plan was short-sighted and shallow, and did far too little to restore order or prosperity to Europe. As a result, many governments were faced with problems they could not solve. And so dictators stepped forward, offering strong rule.

The first of these dictators was Benito Mussolini, who became Italian Prime Minister in 1922. His Fascist Party in their blackshirt uniforms promised to make Italy prosperous at home and respected abroad, and they violently crushed any opposition to their policies. Soon dictators ruled in Austria, Poland, Spain and many other countries of Europe. The most dangerous of them was Adolf Hitler, in Germany.

The Germans had seen the Versailles Treaty as a national humiliation. All Germany's foreign colonies had been taken over by Britain, France, and other countries. And parts of Germany itself had been handed to neighbouring countries. When the Wall Street crash of 1929 plunged Germany into economic crisis, all the bitterness about the Versailles Treaty welled to the surface. And so Germany turned to the Fascist dictator Adolf Hitler and his Nazi Party. By 1933 Hitler was Chancellor, the German equivalent of Prime Minister. Within months he had made Germany a one-party state, and had abolished trade unions and made strikes illegal. Quickly he began to build up Germany's military strength, and then to seize land all around Germany's borders.

Many people in Britain were alarmed by the spread of Fascism in Europe. When a civil war began in Spain in 1936 and Hitler and Mussolini decided to back one side, hundreds of Scots went to Spain to fight against them. The British government decided to begin re-arming in late 1935, but was anxious not to provoke Hitler. So it was not until September 1939 that the crunch came. Hitler attacked Poland despite all warnings, and ignored Britain's ultimatum to pull out. And so on September 3rd 1939 Britain declared war on Germany. The Second World War had begun.

Below A rare colour picture of dictators Hitler and Mussolini together in 1940. *Bottom* A banner calls Scottish workers to the Civil War in Spain.

THOMAS MUIR BAIRD and HARDIE DIED THAT YOU SHOULD BE FREE TO CHOOSE YOUR GOVERNMENT.

WORKERS in SPAIN ARE DYING BECAUSE THEY DARED TO CHOOSE THEIR OWN GOVERNMENT

UNITE FOR THE STRUGGLE!

SPANISH WORKERS DYING FOR DEMOCRA

1938

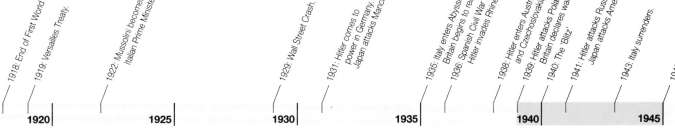

A time-line of world events before and during the Second World War

1918: End of First World War.
1919: Versailles Treaty.
1922: Mussolini becomes Italian Prime Minister.
1929: Wall Street Crash.
1931: Hitler comes to power in Germany. Japan attacks Manchuria.
1935: Italy enters Abyssinia. Britain begins to rearm.
1936: Spanish Civil War begins. Hitler invades Rhineland.
1938: Hitler enters Austria and Czechoslovakia.
1939: Hitler attacks Poland. Britain declares war on Germany.
1940: The 'Blitz'
1941: Hitler attacks Russia. Japan attacks America.
1943: Italy surrenders.
1945: Germany and Japan surrender.

1920   1925   1930   1935   1940   1945

Scotland Goes to War

Evacuation: Children from Canon Mills School, Edinburgh, on their way to Waverley Station on 2nd September 1939, the day before war broke out.

The biggest fear in 1939 was that Britain's cities would be attacked almost immediately by German bombers. So plans had been made to evacuate children from danger areas. By the end of September over a third of Scotland's children had been moved from Glasgow, Edinburgh, Clydebank, Dundee, Rosyth and other places in danger of being bombed. Off they went to halls, schools and houses in Scotland's country areas. It wasn't much fun for many of these young evacuees, separated from their parents and in strange surroundings. Many had not been in the countryside before.

For the people receiving evacuees, it was all strange and new too. For the first time, country people and wealthier people learnt with a shock how poor children in the cities of Scotland normally lived, what they normally ate, what they normally wore. It was becoming clear that this war was going to force everyone closer together and break down a lot of Britain's class barriers.

But 1939 drew to an end and there had been no bombing, no fighting. It was December before the first soldiers were killed. People began to talk about the 'funny war' and the 'Bore war'. Later it became known as the Phoney War. Newspaper sellers began to call out sarcastic headlines: 'Extra: Germans in Berlin, Scotsmen in Aberdeen, read all about it.' Children who had been evacuated started to return, and by Christmas of 1939 three-quarters of them were back at home.

THIS MARKS
THE WRECK OF
H.M.S. ROYAL OAK
AND THE GRAVE OF
HER CREW. RESPECT
THEIR RESTING PLACE.
UNAUTHORISED DIVING
PROHIBITED
BY ORDER OF THE MINISTRY
OF DEFENCE (NAVY)

There was no phoney war at sea. U-boats sank over three quarters of a million tonnes of British shipping in the first nine months of the war.

The Royal Navy started badly too. Once again Scapa Flow in the Orkneys became the main base of Britain's Home Fleet. But it was badly defended. On October 13th 1939 a German submarine commander skilfully took his U-boat right into Scapa Flow, waited until the dead of night, then torpedoed the battleship *Royal Oak*. It sank in minutes and 833 men died.

After the sinking of the *Royal Oak*, great barriers made of concrete blocks and sunken ships were placed across the eastern entrances of Scapa Flow to stop any other U-boats from entering. The barriers were called Churchill Barriers, because they were the idea of Winston Churchill. They are still there, with a road running along the top.

Top Buoy in Scapa Flow *Above* A truck crossing one of the Churchill Barriers. *Right* Winston Churchill outside 10 Downing Street, 1942

For most people in Britain, then, the war was a bit unreal to begin with. It didn't seem to have much to do with them. There were still a million people unemployed in the spring of 1940. In some parts of Scotland, like Dundee, more than one in ten were still unemployed. That didn't make the war effort seem very urgent. And Neville Chamberlain, the Prime Minister, had no clear message about why Britain was at war or what it was fighting for.

Chamberlain's time ran out in May of 1940, when Hitler swept into Norway, taking the British by surprise. Chamberlain resigned, and on the 10th of May Winston Churchill became Prime Minister. Churchill had been warning for years of Hitler's ambitions. Within days he had given the country a goal, a direction, a purpose: 'You ask, What is our policy? I will say: It is to wage war, by sea, land and air, with all our might and with all the strength that God can give us . . . . . You ask, What is our aim? I can answer in one word: Victory – victory at all costs, victory in spite of all terror; victory, however hard and long the road may be.'

Total War

On the very morning of the day that Churchill became Prime Minister, German armies had crossed over the borders of Belgium and Holland. By June France had surrendered. Almost all of Europe was now in the hands of the Nazis. Britain's only supporters were the distant colonies like India, and the Dominions: Australia, Canada, New Zealand and South Africa. America looked on, concerned but unwilling to become involved once more in an European war.

And so Britain mobilized for total war. Everyone became part of the war effort; every aspect of life was devoted to war. The government took almost complete control of industry and transport. Factories like the Rolls-Royce plant at Hillington Industrial Estate west of Glasgow were greatly increased in size, until by 1943 over 20,000 people were working there making aero-engines.

Food was rationed, so that everyone in the country got the same number of vouchers to exchange for food. It was claimed that even King George VI and Queen Elizabeth ate spam . . . off a gold plate. Of course rationing meant that many people got less to eat than they had before the war. But a Scottish scientist called John Boyd Orr had shown in the 1930s that about half the population couldn't afford a proper diet because they didn't earn enough money. So from 1940 rationing meant that a lot of people ate better than they had before. It was the same story with clothes, which were also rationed.

Inside the Rolls-Royce factory at Hillington

No-one was too young or too old to be involved in the war effort. Many older people joined the Home Guard. This became known as 'Dad's Army' and the newspapers ran competitions to find the oldest volunteer. They discovered an ex-regimental sergeant major from Crieff in Perthshire. No-one was sure exactly what age he was, but he had first seen action with the British Army in the Egyptian Campaign in 1884-85!

Wartime ration books

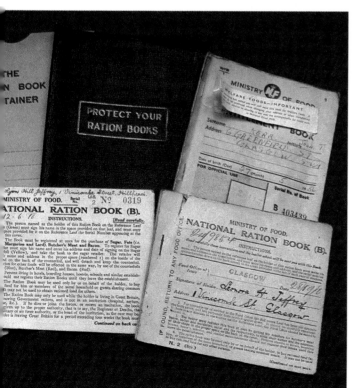

The Home Guard practises a bayonet charge.

Clydeside is Blitzed. An etching by Ian Fleming of a bombing attack.

War in the Air

By the summer of 1940 the 'phoney war' was well and truly over. Hitler had begun preparations to invade Britain. At first he tried to destroy the Royal Air Force, and clear the way for a seaborne landing. Through July, August and September of 1940 the skies of southern England were filled with smoke and vapour trails as the Battle of Britain was fought. Then, when it became clear that the Luftwaffe was not winning, Hitler changed tactics. Now began the 'Blitz'. Hundreds of German bombers would make for the same city and drop incendiary bombs, high explosive bombs, and land mines on the centre and the main industrial areas.

From September to November 1940 London was blitzed every night. Then the raids turned to Britain's other industrial centres. On March 13th 1941 came the first big raids on Clydeside. Over two hundred German bombers left bases stretching from France north to Norway, and by about nine o'clock in the evening had gathered over Clydeside. As the warning sirens began to wail and the first incendiary bombs began to fall, it became obvious that the town of Clydebank was a key target.

Soon fires were blazing at the Yoker distillery at one end of town, the big navy oil storage tanks at the other, and the timber yard of Singer's factory right in the middle. The whole town was lit up perfectly for the bombers. As people sheltered in the entrance ways of their tenement closes, or in corrugated iron shelters in their back gardens, hundreds of tons of high explosives were dropped on Clydebank.

The following night the bombers came back. Fires were still burning from the first raids, and the bombing on the second night was even heavier. When it was all over, and the dead had been dug out from under the rubble, over 1200 people were found to have been killed on Clydeside in these two nights. Over 500 of them had been killed in Clydebank.

The damage to Clydebank's housing was particularly severe. Only 8 of the town's 12,000 houses had escaped damage, and 25,000 of the 47,000 people who lived in the town had been made homeless.

Before the Blitz, many people had believed that these bombing tactics would cripple war industries, demoralize the civilian population, and so lead quickly to an end of the war.

But in fact even big air-raids didn't have much effect on the war effort. The morning after the Clydebank raids quite a few people turned up for work at John Brown's shipyard, having walked through the rubble and smoke to get there. Within a fortnight Clydeside's industries were getting back to normal. It was the same in other British cities that were more badly damaged. 60,000 British civilians, half of them Londoners, were killed during the war by air-raids, but the war effort continued.

Even when Britain made much bigger raids on German cities, using up to a thousand bombers at once and by the end of the war killing perhaps 600,000 German civilians, bombing did not have that effect.

World War

In May 1941 the Blitz on Britain stopped as Hitler laid new plans for his army and airforce. And on June 22nd 1941 these new plans were revealed to the world. Hitler had turned east, and launched an invasion of Russia. Churchill immediately announced Britain's support for Russia. But there was little that Britain could do to help. The main burden of defeating Hitler had been pushed onto Russia.

At the end of 1941 another turning point was reached, and again it was good news for Britain. Japan had been taking advantage of the war in Europe to expand across the Far East. The Americans had blockaded Japan to try to stop this expansion. On December 7th the Japanese tried to break this blockade by attacking the American Pacific naval base of Pearl Harbour. And so America joined the war, committed to defeating first Germany and then Japan.

As the almost limitless strength of America's industries was turned to war production, it became only a matter of time before Germany and Japan faced defeat. The Clyde became one of the main receiving ports for a constantly swelling stream of American war material. Almost two and a half million American troops were disembarked on the Clyde. The airports at Renfrew and

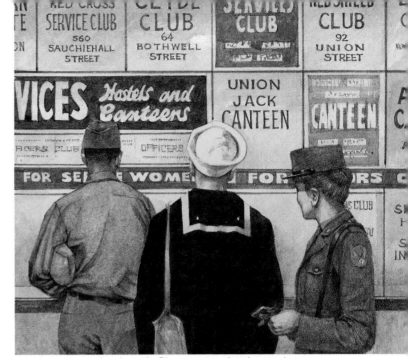

Americans on wartime leave in Glasgow: a modern impression

at Prestwick down the Ayrshire coast became the destination of thousands of aircraft flown straight from their American factories to the European war. And while all this was going on, the British people began to turn their minds to the future, and to think about life when the war was over.

Wartime supplies being handled at Prestwick Airport.

People's War, People's Peace?

Buildings at Peel hospital, built during the war and still in use.

Almost the whole population of Britain was needed during the Second World War. Unemployment vanished for the first time in living memory, and people began to realize that being out of work was not inevitable. Many people had better food. Safety rules for workers were improved. Even the exclusive Gleneagles Hotel had to set aside space in which injured miners could stay while recovering.

These changes happened all over Britain, but some of them went further in Scotland than anywhere else, and one big reason for this was the Secretary of State for Scotland, Tom Johnston. He had been appointed by Churchill in 1941. He was full of energy and ideas, and was given the power to get on and do things. He set up rent tribunals to make sure that rents were fair and that there were no rent strikes as there had been in the Great War. He made sure that war workers and other civilians could use the civil defence hospitals, and that their health was looked after.

And so people began to ask why they should only be looked after during wartime. Why couldn't they have jobs and better housing, food and health in peacetime, too? It was a people's war, so perhaps it should be followed by a people's peace?

The same things had been said during the Great War, and then people had been promised 'a fit land for heroes to live in'. Instead had come the Great Depression and another war. So now people were more determined. They didn't want vague promises and woolly schemes. They wanted concrete plans.

Plans appeared at the end of 1942, drawn up by a former civil servant called Sir William Beveridge. First,

a national scheme run by the government would provide everyone with security, by keeping incomes up to a decent level. Next, disease would have to be dealt with by a National Health Service. This would be a complete system of hospitals, health centres and doctors that anyone in the whole country could use without paying. Finally, the government would have to make sure that mass unemployment was not allowed to return.

Beveridge's plans were not very popular with the wartime government. They worried about what it would all cost and where the money would come from. But most people thought that the Beveridge plan offered a better world. It gave them another reason to work for victory.

The End of the War

Throughout 1943 the Allies gained strength. On the Eastern Front, the Germans had taken a terrible battering from the Russian Red Army, and were being pushed slowly back to Germany. And in the Pacific the Americans were forcing the Japanese off one island after another as they fought to get within bombing range of the Japanese mainland. In Britain, preparations were still being made to open a second front against Hitler by landing an army in occupied France. Material continued to pour across the Atlantic, and by 1944 Prestwick was one of the busiest international airports in the world, receiving a constant stream of American air-cargo.

On June 6th 1944 the invasion of France began, and a huge flotilla of ships crossed the Channel to the beaches of Normandy. It was called Deliverance Day, or D-Day. At last, the Second Front had been opened against Hitler. Now Germany could be squeezed from east and west. On April 30th 1945, Hitler committed suicide, and on 7th May the Germans agreed to an unconditional surrender. The next day church-bells rang throughout Britain.

VE-day (Victory in Europe), May 8th 1945. Edinburgh prepares its party.

DECORATIONS FOR VE DAY IN EDINBURGH STRE

Shopkeepers putting up decorations yesterday in an Edinburgh street.   On right: a colourful display in the

The Japanese city of Hiroshima was completely devastated by an atomic bomb that the Americans dropped on it on August 6th 1945.

The war against Japan continued for three more months. Then on the 6th August 1945 an American plane dropped a single bomb on the Japanese city of Hiroshima. But this was no ordinary bomb. It was an atomic bomb, which killed 60,000 people and injured 100,000. In one instant, it had caused as much death and injury as Britain had experienced from bombing during the whole war. Three days later, on the 9th August, another atomic bomb was dropped on Nagasaki. Again, the destruction was awesome. Japan surrendered on the 14th of August. The Second World War was over, and the nuclear age had begun.

Russia's war-time leader, Stalin, was later asked how the war was won. 'Britain provided time' he said; 'America provided money, and Russia provided blood.'

The American submarine base at Holy Loch, Argyll. The wartime alliance between Britain and America has continued into the present.

The Second World War had been a war of science and of new industries. Jet engines, computers, antibiotics, nuclear power, chemicals and precision engineering had all developed with amazing speed. Before long many of these were in everyday use, like radio and radar in the photograph of an air traffic controller on the right. But at the very time when Scotland might have been getting in on these industries of the future, she turned instead back towards the old heavy industries whose future had been in doubt for years.

Russia had done most of the fighting against Germany, and 20 million Russians had been killed. Poland and Germany had each lost over four million, Japan and Yugoslavia each over one million. Six million Jews had been killed in German extermination camps. In these human terms, Britain escaped fairly lightly. 300,000 British people had been killed in the armed forces, and another 60,000 civilians and 35,000 merchant sailors had been killed. In all, almost 400,000 British people had died, and about 58,000 of them were Scottish.

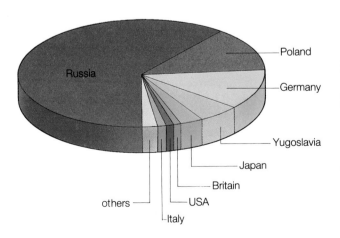

Work to do . . .

1 Write two or three sentences on each of the following, saying who or what they were: the Versailles Treaty; Benito Mussolini; Adolf Hitler; the Phoney War; Winston Churchill.

2 What was the Blitz? What parts of Britain were the main targets? How was Clydebank affected?

3 Explain in your own words what someone might have meant if they had said during the Second World War that the 'people's war' should be followed by a 'people's peace'.

4 Make a list of some of the new inventions and industries that developed during the Second World War. How involved was Scotland in these new activities? What did this have to do with Scotland's future?

Plans and Problems

Choosing a Future

Labour Party election poster, 1945

During the Second World War, many Scots formed strong views on the kind of world they were fighting for. Their chance to make their views known came in July 1945, when Britain held a general election.

Three big issues dominated the election. First, people wanted a big house-building programme to repair the bombing damage and to sweep away the old slums. Second, they wanted a social security system, that would act as a 'safety net' for those who were poor. Third, there was a strong feeling that future governments should prevent unemployment.

For most people it was a straightforward choice between the Conservatives led by Winston Churchill, and the Labour Party led by Clement Attlee. In fact there was a lot of agreement or 'consensus' between them over what should be done. But many people felt that the Conservatives had been to blame for the harsh times before the war. They felt that Labour was more likely to keep its promises.

So when votes were counted, it was found that the Labour Party had won almost 400 seats in the House of Commons, and the Conservative Party not much more than 200. Scotland had voted like the rest of Britain, electing 40 Labour MPs and just 25 Conservatives.

Robert Irvine, a fitter from Edinburgh, was 20 years old when the 1945 election took place. He didn't have a vote, because the voting age was not reduced from 21 to 18 until 1971. But he has very clear memories of the election, and his feelings when the result was announced must have been typical of many Labour supporters:

' . . . we really were over the top, very happy about it . . . One would almost say that you were going to be looked after, and I don't think there was anything wrong about that, for the rest of life; you were going to have ease enough to develop your own characteristics without any of the old anxiety, any of the old poverty. And of course the housing programmes and the industrial reform, all these things were tremendously important . . . So that the '45 election was something which was quite unique in most people's experience and as I say, it led to great hopes, perhaps greater hopes than it should have given rise to.'

Labour in Power

Labour wasted no time in making some big social reforms. By 1948 it had created a much bigger system of social security than had existed ever before. The idea was that the government would collect money by taxing people who could afford to pay, and then pay the money to people who were old, unemployed, sick or poor.

And by 1948 Labour had also set up a National Health Service. The NHS was a way of trying to make sure that people who were sick got proper medical treatment, no matter how rich or poor they might be. The government took over all the hospitals, and made an agreement with all the doctors and dentists and opticians. Anyone needing treatment would get it without having to pay; instead, the government would pay with money raised from taxes.

Many of these post-war reforms, such as the National Health Service, have survived right up to the present. It was after these reforms that people began to describe Britain as a 'welfare state', a country where the government looked after people 'from the cradle to the grave'. But to pay for all this, Britain needed a strong and modern economy. And the fact was that by 1945 the country was almost bankrupt. To pay for the war Britain had run up huge debts, and had almost stopped exporting in order to make war equipment. What would Attlee's Labour government do about the economy?

Labour had two main policies for industry. The first was 'nationalization'. This meant the government taking control of industries that had been privately owned, such as the railways and coalmines. The idea was that by controlling these key industries, which Labour called the 'commanding heights' of the economy, the government could plan the economy. For example it could push industries into certain depressed areas, or keep unemployment down.

Labour's other main policy was an 'export drive': a big effort to increase Britain's exports as much as possible. That would make sure that everyone was kept employed, and would also earn money to import everything that was in short supply or was still rationed.

In some ways, these plans worked very well. Exports soared, and there was hardly any unemployment. Between the wars, one-third of Scotland's miners had been unemployed, but in the first few years after the war there was never more than one in a hundred out of work.

Labour also had some success in directing new industries to Scotland. In 1947 a big new factory for making railway waggons was opened at Linwood by Pressed Steel Fisher. And in Dundee, the government-backed Kingsway Industrial Estate began to attract some big American companies like National Cash Register and Timex.

But Labour's policies had problems, too, especially for Scotland. Scotland's future lay in finding alternatives to the declining heavy industries, whose hey-day was long in the past. Instead, the post-war export drive was making Scotland depend even more on those old industries.

And there was a growing feeling in Scotland that too much control was being moved south of the border. Labour's policies meant central planning, central direction, central control, everything centralised in London.

At the general election in October 1951, many people in Scotland decided not to vote Labour. Labour and Conservative finished up with 35 Scottish seats each, while in the rest of Britain the Conservatives had a majority of seats. Labour were out, now it was the Tories' turn.

Top The nationalization of the coal industry, January 1947 *Right* 'From the cradle to the grave', the Welfare State was meant to help ordinary families like the McKinneys of Edinburgh. This family snapshot shows them in 1947. It includes grandfather at the back, father middle left, grandmother centre, mother bottom left, and son at the front.

The Stone of Destiny Goes Missing

In 1949, a Scottish lawyer called John MacCormick began collecting signatures for a 'Covenant' or petition for a Scottish Parliament. Within a week 50,000 people had signed it, and within a few months almost half a million signatures had been gathered. Then, as the list of signatures continued to grow (it reached two million) another dramatic protest took place. At the centre was Scotland's Stone of Destiny. Nobody knows where Scotland's Stone of Destiny came from, but it is thought to have been brought to Scotland from Antrim in Ireland during the ninth century or even earlier. It was used as Scotland's Coronation stone, on which kings sat when they were crowned. But in 1296 it had been taken from Scone by the English King Edward I, and placed beneath the English throne in Westminster Abbey, London.

Above John MacCormick in 'Kidnapping' stunt, 1951 *Right* 1950, the Stone of Destiny goes missing *Below* The Stone back under the Coronation Chair in Westminster Abbey, London.

Suddenly, on Christmas Day 1950, the Stone went missing. The newspapers were in uproar. The police searched high and low for months, without success. The King, George VI, began to worry: what if he should die and his daughter Elizabeth had to be crowned without the Stone? He was sure that bad luck would befall her, even that the Windsor dynasty would come to an end.

The adventure continued until April 1952, when the Stone was recovered from Arbroath Abbey and taken back to Westminster. Then it was revealed that the Stone had been taken by some Glasgow University students, supported by John MacCormick, in order to attract more attention to the 'Covenant' for a Scottish Parliament.

GUARDIAN, WEDNESDAY, DECEMBER 27, 19[...]

NO TRACE OF MISSING STONE OF DESTINY

Already Over the Border?

POLICE SEARCH FOR MAN AND WOMAN IN CAR

From our London Staff

FLEET STREET, TUESDAY.

Scotland Yard had no further news to-night of the Coronation Stone, the Stone of Scone, or the Stone of Destiny as it is variously called. There is "absolutely no trace" of it, but the police are still busy all over the country—especially on northward routes—looking for it.

The stone was stolen in the early hours of Christmas Day from Westminster Abbey. One theory is that the thieves (or, from the point of view of certain Scotsmen, "liberators") hid in a chapel overnight in readiness for their coup. They had first to prise the stone out of its housing under the Coronation Chair, which is behind the High Altar. Then the stone—which weighs four hundredweight and measures roughly 26in. by 16in. by 11in.—had to be carried round to the Poets' Corner door where, presumably, it was loaded into a car.

SCOTTISH ACCENTS

The police are looking for a man and a woman in a Ford Anglia car, which was seen near the Abbey in the small hours of the morning. Descriptions of them have been circulated, and the police say they speak with Scottish accents. It is taken for granted that the stone has been stolen by Scottish Nationalists.

The stone, which is rectangular and is of yellowish sandstone, has two rings let into it and normally lies behind a grille under the Coronation Chair. In 1940 it was buried in the Abbey, and the secret position marked on a chart which was sent to Canada for safety. It is believed to have left the Abbey

piece of furniture in the Abbey, and has been used for 27 coronations. It wa[s] damaged by the removal of the stone[.] part of it was broken and a strip [of] wood from the grille was found lying [...] the floor.

ALREADY IN SCOTLAND?

Scotland Yard sent a number [of] C.I.D. men, including fingerpri[nt] experts, to the Abbey to-day and ha[ve] circulated a description of the sto[ne.] There is no official confirmation of [the] rumour that a wristlet watch was foun[d] near the Coronation Chair, but it ha[s] been stated that freshly carved initial[s] "J. F. S." have been found in the gildin[g] on the front of the chair.

It seems evident that the intrude[rs] were amateurs, for they made litt[le] attempt to hide their tracks. Whethe[r] or not they will make straight f[or] Scotland with the stone is doubtfu[l] though one Scottish paper said th[is] morning that the stone might alread[y] have crossed the border. It should no[t] prove a difficult object to hide onc[e it] can be taken out of the car which [is] carrying it, and the police of the tw[o] countries are likely to find themselve[s] with a difficult job—not so much in find[ing] the culprits but in finding the ston[e.] If anybody is brought to court either o[n] a charge of stealing or of sacrilege, th[e] case should produce some fine legal an[d] historical points.

WATCHMAN "ALONE IN THE ABBEY"

Mr Andrew Hislop (48), night watch[-] man-fireman at the Abbey, told [a] reporter last night how he discovere[d] that the stone was missing:

"I was quite alone in the Abbey. Th[...]

[left partial column:]
[...]ions
[...]r of
been
They
[...] the
[...]ave
[...]sider
[...] the
[...]een
[...]wn
[...]tinct
and

that
[...]ying
[...]line
[...] pro-
[...]joint
[...]pose

[...]olicy
[...] and
[...]y it
[...]s of
[...]ting
[...]ore
[...] all
[...]ting
[...] not

Indian Summer, or Fool's Paradise

Above Harold MacMillan grouse shooting in Aberdeenshire in 1958 *Below* 'You've never had it so good': modern living in 1960.

The 1950s were an Indian Summer for Scotland's old industries, a late spell of unexpectedly good fortune. There was no competition from Germany and Japan, who were still rebuilding their war-torn industries, and so Scotland's industries found it easy to export. Unemployment almost vanished: during the 1950s only 3 in every 100 Scottish workers were looking for a job.

Rationing and shortages ended too, and in place of the 'age of austerity', people began to talk of the 'affluent society'. With everything going so well, the Conservatives won easily another general election in 1955. In Scotland 36 of the 71 seats were won by the Conservatives, the only time they have ever won a majority of Scottish seats.

By the late 1950s it was becoming normal for families to own consumer goods like a car, television, washing-machine, refrigerator and record player. It was all a far cry from the Depression or war-time. When

the Conservative leader Harold Macmillan said in 1959 'you've never had it so good,' many people agreed with him and gave him the credit. That year the Conservatives won their third general election in a row.

But Scotland's Indian Summer was coming to an end. By the late 1950s countries like Germany and Japan had had over ten years to rebuild their war-torn industries. Now they were modern, efficient, and ready to work hard for success. They made things that people wanted to buy, and did so cheaply and reliably.

In contrast, Scotland clung to its old industries, its old factories and machines, its old attitudes and work-practices. And as a result, one after another, these industries collapsed.

A typical example was Glasgow's North British Locomotive Company. It had a long history of exporting steam engines around the world. But railways were switching to diesel and electric locomotives. North British were slow off the mark and when they did produce a diesel engine it did not work very well. By 1963 it was out of business, and 5,000 jobs had vanished.

Other famous companies went the same way. The glare of Dixon's iron-works – 'Dixon's Blazes' – which had lit up Glasgow's night sky for generations, faded into darkness. Tennant's chemical factory in north-east Glasgow, once one of the largest in the world, was bull-dozed away.

As this collapse began, the old problem of unemployment returned to Scotland. In just one year, from 1958 to 1959, the number of Scots out of work doubled from 58 thousand to 116 thousand. Scotland's Indian Summer was at an end. So little had been done about the country's industrial problems, that some people began to wonder if Scotland had really been living in a Fool's Paradise.

Time for a Change

By 1960, Prime Minister Harold Macmillan had decided that the Conservatives would have to change policy. Instead of leaving private companies to open factories wherever they wanted, the government began to push them towards areas like Scotland where unemployment was increasing.

This new policy soon produced results. In 1961 the British Motor Corporation was given government help to open a truck and tractor factory at Bathgate. Two years later the Rootes car company was encouraged to open a car factory at Linwood near Paisley. And in the west Highlands, the Wiggins Teape company was given government help to open a paper mill in Fort William.

These new factories created thousands of new jobs, and the government promised that thousands more were 'in the pipeline'.

But the government also lost support in Scotland when it was announced in 1963 that many of the country's railway lines were losing money and should be closed. What's more, their new leader Sir Alec Douglas-Home, who was the MP for Kinross and West Perthshire, seemed a bit old-fashioned. The Labour Party led by Harold Wilson seemed more up-to-date. It talked about modernising Britain with 'the white heat of the technological revolution'. It talked about the need to plan Britain's future. It talked about the 'thirteen wasted Tory years'.

So when a general election was held in 1964, the Conservatives did especially badly in Scotland and lost 7 MPs. Labour scraped into power with a tiny majority, and the Wilson years had begun.

The Duke of Edinburgh visits the Rootes car factory, Linwood in 1963.

Labour's Plans for Scotland

Harold Wilson visiting Ayr in 1968.

The Conservatives had begun the fashion for planning, but Labour went much further. In 1965 the government published a National Plan for Britain. This contained a long list of things that the government hoped would happen over the next five years: faster economic growth, more jobs, better management.

Next, the government set up the Highlands and Islands Development Board, which it hoped would help industry to grow in the north of Scotland. Then at the beginning of 1966 the government published a detailed plan for all Scotland. It was called the Plan for Expansion, and it painted a rosy picture of Scotland's future. Government money would be poured into new roads, schools, houses, hospitals and universities. Industry would be given government money to build new factories and create more jobs. People would be given training for new industries like electronics. In all, Scotland would get two thousand million pounds of government money over the five years of the plan.

Labour's plans for the future created a lot of interest and excitement. So when they decided to hold another general election in the spring of 1966, their majority leapt from just 4 to almost 100 MPs.

But other things were going badly for Labour. Britain had for several years been importing more than she was exporting. Instead of taking action to tackle the problem, the government dithered. People abroad lost confidence in it, and in the summer of 1966 it was forced to take drastic steps. Wages and prices were all 'frozen', and government spending was cut. So Scotland's Plan for Expansion, only a few months old, was left in ruins.

Problems for Labour

Left A show of hands at a mass meeting outside the Linwood car factory in 1966. *Inset* The SNP symbol *Below* Winnie Ewing wins the Hamilton by-election in 1967.

Labour's changes of policy caused a lot of anger. They had raised hopes high and then dashed them. As unemployment rose sharply, 1966 became one of the worst years on record for emigration from Scotland. About 50,000 people decided to pack up and leave.

Labour faced other problems too. Scotland's older industries were slipping ever deeper into trouble. Many coal pits and shipyards were losing money.

Some of the new industries that were meant to offer Scotland a bright future were also in trouble. The motor factories at Linwood and Bathgate had half empty order books, and relations between the management and the assembly-line workers were terrible. At Linwood there were over 300 strikes in just 6 years between 1963 and 1969. Once there were 6 strikes in 9 days.

In this gloomy atmosphere the Scottish National Party began to make news. Its membership had been soaring, from 2,000 in 1962 to 40,000 by 1966. Its simple message, 'Put Scotland First', was winning it support in local council elections.

Then in 1967 there had to be a by-election to find a new MP for Hamilton. The Scottish Nationalists put forward as their candidate Mrs Winifred Ewing, a Glasgow solicitor who was a good speaker and a good campaigner. And when the by-election was held on November 2nd, 'Winnie' demolished Labour's huge majority and won Hamilton with almost 2,000 votes to spare. The SNP had a member of Parliament.

At first Labour panicked at the sensational success of the Scottish Nationalists. But it had soon begun to fight back. Plans were announced in 1968 to build a new aluminium smelter at Invergordon on the Moray Firth. Also in 1968, the government moved the National Savings Bank from England to Glasgow.

Then there was the electronics industry. During the 1960s the number of Scots working in electronics jumped from just 8 thousand to over 30 thousand. Some of these jobs came from foreign companies, like the American computer giant IBM, which had a factory near Greenock. Others came from British companies like Ferranti, with a large factory in Edinburgh.

So by the end of the 1960s Labour could claim that it was doing quite a lot for Scotland. Hundreds of millions of pounds were being spent to help industry. Education, transport, and the health service were all getting extra money. By 1969 the government was spending twenty per cent more on each Scot than on each English person. This made it hard for the Scottish Nationalists to argue that Scotland would be better off independent, and their support began to fade.

On the other hand, some people began to accuse the Labour government of wasting money, of propping up old industries that had no future. And at the centre of this argument was the symbol of Scotland's heavy industry – shipbuilding.

Decline on the Clyde

The shipyards of the Clyde were in deep trouble by the 1960s. The Clyde had specialised in building passenger ships, while passengers all over the world were turning to air travel. The great ocean liners were luxurious, but compared with the new airliners they were expensive and slow.

The way ships were built on the Clyde was also falling behind the rest of the world. Far too little had been spent in modernizing the yards.

James Glendinning was a shipwright in the yards:

'I was once part of a trade union delegation to Sweden, away about 1965, and I was amazed at the progress that was apparent in Sweden. For example, there wasn't such a thing as launching the vessel; their berths were dry docks which were roofed in so that even in the severe winters of Sweden the men were able to work under cover . . . the working conditions were vastly superior to anything we had here . . . And instead of the hassle there is here, with launching ways, and check chains and so on, you simply opened the dock gates and the vessel was floated out. Miles, years and years ahead of British shipbuilding.'

James Glendinning also has many memories of demarcation disputes that caused so much trouble in Scottish shipyards:

'I think a classical example of that was a port-hole – a porthole in a vessel. You would have, in the first instance . . . a shipwright that would mark the holes for burning and the burner would come up and burn the hole out. And then you would get a caulker, or rather the shipwright would then mark the holes for fastening the portlight. Then the driller would come and drill the holes, and then the caulker would come back and bolt it together. Well there was a lot of time wasting because one trade was waiting for another . . . each trade jealously guarded their own work, because of the fact that they'd went through a depression, no work, and they were going to make sure that nobody took any work away from them . . . So that it was pretty bitter at times.'

And the workforce was divided into dozens of different trade unions. The plumbers and the painters, the electricians and engineers, the welders and riveters, the boilermakers and the joiners were each in a different union. This led to a lot of arguments over who should do what, arguments that were known as demarcation disputes.

Looking back, it is easy to see that these problems on the Clyde were a recipe for disaster. More and more countries, like Germany, Japan and South Korea, were able to built ships faster and more cheaply. But at the time it was hard for anyone to change. People were locked into old ways. It was a bit like the kind of play called a Greek tragedy, a gripping drama where events can only lead to disaster.

Lame Ducks and U-turns

In 1968, with shipyards all along the Clyde collapsing, the Labour government decided to act. All the yards on the upper reaches of the Clyde were brought together into one big concern: Upper Clyde Shipbuilders, or UCS.

Upper Clyde Shipbuilders had an unhappy and short life. All the old problems were very much in evidence. There was the aloof and distant management, the bowler-hatted foremen and gaffers. There was trouble between unions about demarcation, and a strike record almost as bad as that in car factories like Linwood.

In 1969, when John Brown launched the last great Cunarder ever to be built on the Clyde, the *Queen Elizabeth II*, a surge of the old pride was felt along the river.

But Upper Clyde Shipbuilders had lost money in building the *QEII*, and was also losing money on other ships it was building.

1971: UCS workers, listening to Jimmy Reid, decide to hold a work-in.

'UCS: Defend Your Right To Work' banner

In 1970 the Labour government had to come to the rescue again, and UCS received twenty million pounds to help it. But later that year, Labour lost a general election to the Conservatives led by Edward Heath.

The Conservatives argued that industries had to learn to stand on their own feet, and stop coming to the government for hand-outs. In future, said the new government, 'lame duck' industries would not be getting any help. So in June 1971, when UCS asked for another six million pounds to cover its losses, the government said no. Six thousand of the UCS's eight and a half thousand jobs would have to go.

The unions knew that if they went on strike the yards would be closed as soon as they walked out. So they occupied the yards and said that they would run the yards themselves until the government backed down.

'This is the first campaign of its kind in trade unionism' said Jimmy Reid, a Communist shop steward and one of the main union leaders. 'We are not going on strike. We are not even having a sit-in. We do not recognise that there should be any redundancies and we are going to *work*-in. We are taking over the yards because we refuse to accept that faceless men can make these decisions. . . . They have taken on the wrong people and we will fight.'

The UCS 'work-in' was a great way of attracting publicity. A fighting fund was started and almost a quarter of a million pounds was given to it by the public. There were marches, strikes, concerts, and records in support of the work-in. Finally, in February 1972, the government admitted defeat. UCS would stay open. One yard, John Brown, would be sold to the American company Marathon. The other three yards, renamed Govan Shipbuilders, would get £35 million of taxpayers' money. The work-in had worked.

Edward Heath's government was badly damaged by the UCS work-in. It had been forced to reverse its policy of giving no help to 'lame ducks'. It had done a somersault or 'U-turn', and that had made it seem weak and aimless. Soon afterwards, it was forced to make more U-turns in its policies. And other groups of workers, like the coalminers in 1972, found that they, too, could defeat the government.

By 1973, the government had lost a lot of public support. But Labour were not doing much better. It seemed that many people were becoming fed up with Conservative *and* Labour, and were beginning to support other parties. In England, the Liberal Party started winning a lot more support. And in Scotland, the Scottish National Party began to grow again. What's more, the SNP had a completely new weapon – North Sea oil.

Work to do . . .

1 What were the main issues in the general election of 1945? Which party won the election? What big social reforms did it make? What were its main industrial policies?
2 Explain why some people described the 1950s as an 'Indian Summer' for Scotland's traditional industries.
3 What was the 'Plan for Expansion'? Who made it, and when? What happened to it?
4 Describe the ups and downs of the SNP during the 1960s.
5 Here are some words and phrases that were in popular use during the 1960s and 1970s: demarcation disputes; lame duck industries; work-ins; U-turns. What did these mean?

Into the Present

The Black Black Oil

The world's oil companies had become interested in the North Sea after a huge field of natural gas was found along the coast of Holland in 1959. As the drilling barges and rigs began to creep northwards, they found more gas in giant fields off the coast of East Anglia. Nearly all the gas we use comes from these fields, and is pumped through a network of pipelines that stretches across Britain.

Then in 1969 Phillips Petroleum discovered the first big oilfield. It was called Ekofisk, and it was in Norwegian waters. It was a long way north of the gas fields in water that was much deeper and rougher. But it was such a big find that all the other oil companies also began to move their search further north.

In 1970 British Petroleum hit the jackpot when they found the first big oilfield in British waters. Called the Forties field, it was almost two hundred kilometres north-east of Aberdeen. And in 1971 another huge field called Brent was discovered even further north, in the wild deep seas east of Shetland.

Soon a long string of oil-fields had been found in the British waters of the North Sea. There were Argyll and Auk in the south, then Montrose and Forties, Piper and Claymore, Beryl and Frigg, on northwards to Ninian and Heather, Cormorant and Thistle.

Key

- ● Oil/Gas field
- ⬯ Oil terminal
- ⚓ Fabrication yard
- —— Oil pipeline
- —— Gas pipeline

(Map of Scotland and the North Sea showing oil and gas fields, terminals, fabrication yards and pipelines. Labels include: Magnus, Thistle, Cormorant, Brent, Heather, Ninian, SHETLAND ISLANDS, Sullom Voe, Lerwick, Frigg, Beryl, NORTH SEA, ORKNEY ISLANDS, Kirkwall, Flotta, Thurso, Wick, Claymore, Piper, Beatrice, Invergordon, Nigg, Moray Firth, Ardersier, Inverness, Loch Kishorn, St. Fergus, Forties, Montrose, Aberdeen, Fort William, Montrose, Arbroath, Fulmar, Auk, Argyll, Dundee, Loch Fyne, Methil, Grangemouth, Glasgow, Edinburgh. Scale bar: 0 50 100 150 km.)

'It's Scotland's Oil!'

When oil was discovered off the Scottish coast in 1970, the Scottish National Party was among the first to see its importance. The oil industry would create tens of thousands of jobs: jobs building ships and rigs and pipelines, jobs supplying the rigs, jobs in oil refineries, jobs for scientists and pilots, divers and welders. And with North Sea oil, there would be no need to buy oil from abroad. The country would save a fortune on its import bill. The government could raise another fortune by taxing the oil companies.

All in all, here was a golden opportunity to rebuild the economy and modernise the whole country. But the Scottish National Party took the view that unless Scotland was independent, England would benefit and Scotland would lose out. And so at the beginning of 1973 the SNP launched their most famous campaign, under the slogan 'It's Scotland's Oil!'

110

THE TIMES
BUSINESS NEWS

BP strikes sea oil

British Petroleum is believed to have found oil in its latest well, in the North Sea off Aberdeen.

It is not known yet if the find is commercial or how significant it is. BP has been drilling for several weeks in the area. Recently a group headed by the American firm Phillips Petroleum made a significant find, the first in the British sector.

They could not have picked a better moment. In October 1973 the Middle East erupted in war. As the fighting spread, the arab oil-states of the region decided that the time had come to teach the world a lesson. First, they suddenly made big cuts in their oil exports. Then, as shortages began, they announced big increases in the price of oil. In just a few months, the price doubled then doubled again.

Oil was suddenly at the centre of world politics. For many countries, the soaring oil prices were bad news. Their import bills shot up, leaving them less money to spend on other things. But for Britain, more expensive oil was quite good news. It made North Sea oil that much more valuable. And with oil prices so high, even the smallest North Sea oilfields in the deepest waters might make a profit.

The SNP had been the first party to make oil a big issue, and in 1974 they got their reward. In February of that year, faced with an all-out strike by the coal miners, Edward Heath held a general election. It produced no clear winner, but the Scottish National Party increased their MPs from one to seven.

In an effort to find a definite winner, another general election took place in October. And this time Labour emerged with a tiny but clear majority. Once again, Harold Wilson was Prime Minister. But the SNP had again done very well. Three in ten voters in Scotland had supported it, and as a result it had increased its MPs from seven to eleven.

For the first time in history, the SNP had become a force that the government could not afford to ignore.

It's Scotland's Oil

Top left Oil crisis in 1973, and cars queue for petrol *Top right* The first oil finds are reported: news, but not yet big news *Above* SNP slogan *Left* SNP officials and MPs line up on Edinburgh Castle Esplanade in March 1974 to celebrate their general election gains.

111

By 1974, the race to bring North Sea oil ashore was in full swing. The Forties field was leading the race. It was so big that four platforms had to be built to bring the oil to the surface. Then a pipeline was laid from these platforms along the seabed to Cruden Bay, which was over a hundred and sixty kilometres away on the coast north of Aberdeen. From there, another pipeline was laid overland to the oil refinery at Grangemouth, over two hundred kilometres away.

The oil meant jobs for thousands of people. But less than a quarter of the work had been won by British companies. An American company designed all four platforms for the Forties field, and built two of them. The steel for the platforms came from Japan, France and Scandinavia. The pipelines were made in Japan, and were laid by Italian and American companies.

So in 1974 the government made it clear that it expected as many as possible of the platforms to be built in Britain. Sites where there was enough room to build these monsters were made ready.

And so in 1975, when another sixteen platforms were ordered by the oil companies for the British North Sea, ten of the orders came to Britain.

The number of jobs created in Scotland by the oil industry was also rising fast. At first, much of the work was created by big construction projects. At Sullom Voe on Shetland, three thousand workers were needed to build a giant oil terminal. And at the Loch Kishorn platform site, the workforce at one point soared to four thousand.

Left An oil pipeline snakes over Scotland's countryside, ready to be buried. *Above* A huge platform for the Beryl oilfield takes shape at Methil in Fife. The other main platform sites in Scotland were on the west coast at Loch Kishorn in Applecross, and on the east coast at Nigg on the Cromarty Firth and Ardersier on the Moray Firth.

But building the platforms was just the first step. It was soon clear that keeping them running would create far more jobs. The platforms needed crews of up to 250 people. The crews had to be flown back and forward on helicopters. Food and equipment had to be taken out on supply ships. Divers were needed for underwater work. And so much money was at stake that the whole complicated business had to be run smoothly from a headquarters.

An oil supply ship enters Aberdeen harbour.

This kind of work gave a boost to ports all along the east coast. Dundee, Peterhead, and Fraserburgh harbours all picked up work from the oil supply boats. At Montrose, the old fishing village of Ferryden on the River South Esk was swept aside to create a forty-acre service base, with quays, cranes, warehouses, workshops and offices. And ahead of all the others, Aberdeen became the centre of Britain's North Sea oil industry. Its harbour boomed, its airport boomed, its industrial estates boomed. House and office prices rocketed as people and companies flocked to Aberdeen, the 'oil capital'.

In 1972 just three thousand people worked in Scotland's infant oil industry, but by 1976 the number was fifty thousand and still rising.

A Scottish Assembly

In 1977, Prime Minister Callaghan (above) spoke of a bright future. 'God', he said, 'has given Britain her best opportunity for one hundred years in the shape of North Sea oil.'

In 1975 the first North Sea Oil was brought ashore. And it was soon clear that there was enough oil under the North Sea for all Britain's needs. By 1980 Britain would be an oil exporter. This was good news for the Labour government led by James Callaghan. He had become Prime Minister in 1976, after Harold Wilson had caused a great surprise by resigning with very little warning.

But a tide of troubles was growing around James Callaghan's government. Despite the new jobs in the oil industry, unemployment in Scotland doubled. Labour had also put up taxes and cut government spending. So it was no surprise when it began losing by-elections. By 1977, its majority of four MPs had vanished.

To stay in power without a majority, Labour needed friends in other parties. More than ever, it had to take notice of the eleven Scottish National Party MPs. And so Labour pushed on with its plans to set up a Scottish Assembly in Edinburgh. The Assembly would have 142 members who would be elected every four years. It would look after some things like housing and education, but the government at Westminster would keep control of things like taxes, defence and foreign policy. So, the Assembly fell a long way short of home rule for Scotland. But it looked like being more powerful than local government.

Some people thought it would be too powerful, others that it would be too weak. Some people didn't think it would work at all, others just could not understand all the complex details.

The Assembly would need somewhere to meet, and the old Royal High School on Calton Hill in Edinburgh was chosen (below).

As workmen began converting the building, the arguments about the Assembly continued.

The Referendum: It's Britain's Oil

Before passing a law to create the Assembly, the government agreed to hold a 'referendum'. The Assembly would go ahead only if at least forty per cent of all Scots voters turned out and voted in favour.

Only thirty-three per cent turned out and voted Yes, well short of the forty per cent needed.

Why was the Assembly not supported? first, people in many parts of the country felt that an Assembly would spend all its time dealing with the problems of Glasgow and Edinburgh, and would ignore the rest of Scotland. There was a strong 'No' vote in areas like the Borders. In Shetland people were saying that if Scotland broke away from England, Shetland would break away from Scotland!

REGION / ISLANDS AREA	YES VOTES	NO VOTES
WESTERN ISLES	6,218	4,933
DUMFRIES & GALLOWAY	27,162	40,239
SHETLAND ISLANDS	2,020	5,466
CENTRAL	71,296	59,105
FIFE	86,252	74,436
ORKNEY ISLANDS	2,104	5,439
BORDERS	20,746	30,780
TAYSIDE	91,482	93,325
GRAMPIAN	94,944	101,485
LOTHIAN	187,221	186,421
STRATHCLYDE	596,519	508,599
HIGHLAND	44,973	43,274
TOTAL	1,230,937	1,153,502

The referendum result is announced, 1st March 1979

Second, support for the SNP was beginning to fade away. More and more people found it hard to see what an Assembly could do about problems like unemployment without any powers over the economy. And slogans like 'It's Scotland's Oil', or 'Rich Scots or poor British' had begun to sound selfish and small-minded, even to people in the SNP.

Third, Labour had been split, with some Labour MPs like Tam Dalyell very strongly against an Assembly. And the Labour government had its mind on other things anyway. It had fallen out with the trade unions, and over the winter there had been one strike after another. People were talking about the 'winter of discontent' and wondering what Prime Minister Callaghan would do.

But whatever the reasons, the Scottish Assembly had been stopped, and Scottish voters had stopped it.

Conservative Party election poster, 1979

The end of the Assembly was also the end of James Callaghan's Labour government. A few weeks after the referendum, the Scottish Nationalist MPs led a vote of no-confidence in the government, which was forced to hold a general election in May 1979.

In Scotland Labour did quite well. They finished the election with forty-four MPs, double the number that the Conservatives had. The big losers in Scotland were the Scottish Nationalists, who started the election with eleven MPs and ended up with only two.

But the Scottish results were no guide to the rest of Britain. In England, Labour suffered a crushing defeat, and the Conservatives won a big majority. Britain had a new Prime Minister: Margaret Thatcher.

Into the Eighties

Margaret Thatcher had replaced Edward Heath as Conservative leader in 1975. She was determined that her government would not be like his. There would be no more U-turns, she said, no emergency rescues of lame ducks. And if the unions wanted to fight, she would be ready to fight back.

In the first few years after 1979 almost every industry in Britain found the going very tough. It was hard to export, sales at home were poor, and competition from abroad was fierce. All over the country factories laid off workers or closed down, and unemployment began to soar. During 1980 and 1981 there were big job losses in Scotland almost every week: at Weirs in Cathcart, ICI in Ayrshire, Rolls-Royce in Hillington, Hoover in Cambuslang, Dunlop in Renfrew.

Whole factories vanished, like the Singer works at Clydebank, once one of the largest factories in Europe. Industries that previous governments had moved to Scotland found it impossible to continue without support: the aluminium smelter at Invergordon closed in 1982; the pulp mill at Corpach by Fort William closed. In the biggest closure of all, the car factory at Linwood closed in 1981, leaving 4,800 people without work.

Margaret Thatcher electioneering in Scotland in 1979

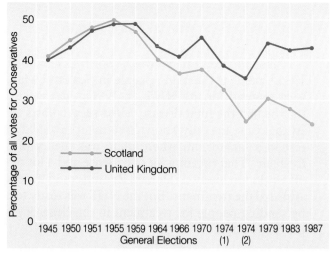
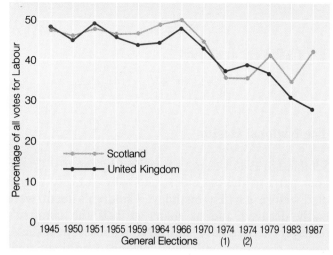

Above How Scotland votes. In recent elections Scotland has not voted in the same way as the United Kingdom as a whole.

During these grim years, Margaret Thatcher's government faced storms of criticism. But its answer was always the same: 'There Is No Alternative'. It claimed that the collapse of old and inefficient industries could no longer be avoided. They had to make way for new industries, new jobs. And when it called a general election in 1983, it won easily. English voters, it seemed, had agreed that there was no alternative, even if the Scots had again elected twice as many Labour MPs as Conservatives.

After 1983, there were some signs of renewal. Some people pointed to the electronics industry, to the IBM factory at Greenock, to the new factories being built by fast-growing companies such as Wang, Digital, and Compaq. By 1987 data processing equipment was Scotland's biggest export. Other people pointed to the growth of Edinburgh as Europe's second largest centre for banking, insurance, and finance. In many parts of the country there were signs of old warehouses and factories being cleaned, repaired, and converted to new uses. And the Scottish Development Agency, set up in 1975 to help Scottish industry and improve Scotland's environment, was envied by many other countries.

The IBM factory in Spanga Glen near Greenock employed three thousand people making personal computers in 1988.

But for most Scots, these changes were not enough. Too many people were still unemployed. Too many factories continued to close. Even the oil industry, once such a bright hope, had a bad time after world oil prices collapsed at the end of 1985. When Margaret Thatcher led the Conservatives for a third time into a general election in 1987, the Scots gave a massive vote of no confidence in her, and elected only 10 Conservative but 50 Labour MPs. Even so, she swept back to power with a big majority in England, and so Scotland's future remained firmly in Conservative hands. No-one could predict what that future might hold: but for the moment, there was no alternative.

Work to do . . .

1 The oil industry has brought jobs and wealth to Scotland. It has also brought many new words and phrases. Find out what these mean: toolpushers; roustabouts; blow-outs; dry holes. Then try to discover other words and phrases used in the oil industry and add them to the list.
2 'It's Scotland's Oil!' was the SNP slogan that caused a lot of argument during the 1970s. Do you agree or disagree with it? Why?
3 When was the referendum on a Scottish Assembly held? Would you have voted for or against it? Why?
4 The referendum on the Scottish Assembly was an unusual event for Britain, but some countries have lots of referendums on all sorts of topics. Can you think of some topic on which you would like a referendum to be held? Try to hold a referendum in your class, with ballot papers, a voting booth, people to count the votes and a 'returning officer' to read out the result.
5 Draw up a list of companies, factories, or industries that have closed or shrunk in your area in the past few years. Make another list of any that have opened or grown. Then compare the two lists, and write down what you think they show.

Home Life

The National Health

Scotland in 1945 was not a very healthy country. In the poor parts of the big cities, one baby in every twelve died before its first birthday. Children's teeth were badly decayed and as many as half the country's teenagers needed false teeth. Damp houses, poor diets, smoky chimneys and bad working conditions took their toll on adults. The first big post-war change was the National Health Service, which was set up in 1948. The NHS aimed to provide the best possible medical care to everyone. There would be no charge for treatment, for the money needed to run the service would be raised from taxes.

There was nothing quite like it anywhere else in the world and it quickly proved to be immensely popular. For the first time, many people could get the glasses or false teeth they had needed for years. Gradually new hospitals were built, and more doctors and nurses were trained.

Better treatment was not the only thing that improved Scotland's health after the war. Some big steps were taken to prevent diseases like whooping cough and measles by a 'jab' or 'jag' that immunised them. People were encouraged to have their chest x-rayed so that TB could be spotted before it became too serious.

Donald Renton, who was born in Portobello in 1925, is one of the many people in Scotland who feel very grateful for the NHS. In 1951 it was discovered that he had the lung disease called tuberculosis or TB. At that time the only known treatment involved a long rest in a sanatorium where there was plenty of clean fresh air. That meant a lot of expense and a lot of time off work. On his own, Donald Renton could never have afforded the treatment. But the NHS was ready to help by sending people for treatment in the clean dry air of the Swiss Alps:

'. . . I was very lucky in, I think the date was 1954 . . . there was a special unit in Davos Wolfgang in Switzerland for Scotsmen only and Scots ladies, like, you know. So, I was sent out to Switzerland, anyway, and I was there for fourteen months, basically that was lying in bed most of the time but I had an operation there . . . I had some surgery there which fortunately eventually done the trick for me, you know. . . . and of course, I have the National Health Service to thank for that. And once again I would say that it's my, well, it's been a proven opinion of course that without nationalisation of medicine like all these things, we would still be in the Dark Ages in this country, you know, and they, they, that sort o' allowed me to, to get a cure which I possibly would not have had without them, you know.'

Left A heavy smog lies over Greenock in the 1950s *Right* A 1975 photograph shows big improvements

Another of Scotland's big health hazards was air pollution. Thick clouds of sooty smoke poured out of chimneys and settled in a foggy blanket over Scotland's towns and cities. In winter the fog turned into a dense and poisonous 'smog'.

Cars and buses were forced to creep slowly along the kerbs. People on the pavements coughed and spluttered and bumped into each other. Buildings were blackened, and so were people's lungs.

In 1956 the government at last took some action, and passed the Clean Air Act. Slowly, this transformed the atmosphere. 'Smokeless zones' were created, where people could burn coal in their fires only if it was smokeless.

Factories were forced to clean up the belching chimney stacks. Gradually the fogs and smogs disappeared, and people found that they could breathe more easily.

Queueing for tuberculosis X-rays in Edinburgh, 1955

Old people being cared for in the Royal Victoria Hospital, Edinburgh.

Compared to people in England and many countries in Europe, the Scots are still not very healthy. But Scotland is a far healthier place to be born and live than it was forty years ago. Fewer than one in a hundred babies now die before their first birthday. Boys and girls grow taller. No-one needing treatment has to worry about being able to afford it.

Perhaps the biggest change is that people now live longer. In 1950 the average life of a Scottish woman spanned 68 years, and a man lived for around 64 years. But by 1985 a woman could expect to live until she was 76, and a man until he was 70. So there are now more old people in Scotland than ever before. Giving people a longer life has been a great achievement, but older people need help and care, with good hospitals and special homes. For many years into the future, one of Scotland's biggest tasks will be to make sure that longer lives are well worth living.

What Scots die of

Cancer (21%)

Other causes (21%)

Heart diseases (35%)

Strokes (15%)

Accidents and violence (5%)

Bronchitis and other chest diseases (3%)

Healthier Scots

Average length of life in Scotland.

76
70
69
64
1986
1951
53
56
1921
46
44
1885

How Scotland's health compares

Cancer

Strokes

Scotland

England

Coronary heart disease

0   50   100   150   200

Rate of death amongst every 100,000 adults.

15%
1890
1914
10%
1933
5%
1948
1986
0%

Percentage of Scots children dying before their first birthday.

117

School Questions

Education was one Scottish industry that grew after 1945. But there were also growing worries about Scotland's schools, and more arguments about the kind of education Scotland needed for the future.

Changes began in 1947, when the school leaving age was raised to fifteen. An extra year in school was meant to be a chance to learn more, but in practice it did not always seem like that.

Jackie Stewart was born in 1939, and went to school near Milton in Dumbartonshire. He remembers school in the 1940s and 1950s as:

. . . 'the unhappiest period of my life. I hear parents constantly saying to their children and to young people in general, 'you'll never have it so good. You'll look back with fond memories. You'll realise in later years how lucky you were to have the camaraderie school provides.' For me, none of those things is true.

When I was young, almost from the very beginning as I remember it, school hung over me like a thunder cloud. I simply was not a good student. In fact I was very poor in the learning process. In the end I was considered dumb, stupid and thick because I could not keep up with the rest of the children in whatever class I was in. It was therefore with great relief to all concerned when, at fifteen, I was able to part company with my formal education and go to work in a garage.'

In fact Jackie Stewart went on to a life of great success. From that garage in Milton he became a motor racing driver and three times World Champion in 1969, 1971 and 1973. But looking back on his schooldays, he still feels annoyed

'that people did not realize that maybe there was something in Jackie Stewart which would allow him to learn, if they used a different method of teaching.'

During the 1950s it was very common to leave school aged fifteen, without qualifications, and with relief. Less than one in ten pupils stayed on. Even fewer went on to study in a technical college or a university.

It did not bode well for Scotland's future. Scotland had been well served in the past by her schools and universities. But changes were needed to keep up with the outside world.

In 1962 a new exam called the 'O'-grade was introduced, so that more people would be able to get a qualification before leaving school. And in 1965 it was decided to turn all the local secondary schools into comprehensives. No longer would children be sent to 'junior' or 'senior' schools according to how well they

Above Jackie Stewart, World Champion: 'school hung over me like a thunder cloud' *Below* Cranhill Secondary School library in 1961

did in an exam at the end of primary school. Instead, everyone from the same area would go to the same school.

While these changes were happening in the schools, the number of universities in Scotland was doubled. The ancient universities of St. Andrews, Glasgow, Aberdeen and Edinburgh were joined by four newcomers: Dundee, Strathclyde, Heriot-Watt and Stirling.

Stirling University was built on a beautiful woodland site a few miles ouside Stirling. It was Scotland's first 'campus' university, with shops, flats, sport, and art centres, pubs, a library and teaching blocks all brought together in its grounds.

As a result of these changes, more people left school with qualifications, and there was more opportunity to go on to college or university. But during the 1970s a lot of new doubts bubbled up to the surface. Why was Scotland one of the last countries in Europe where teachers were allowed to punish pupils with a leather belt or strap? Why did so few working-class people reach university?

And many pupils still found it hard to see why they were at school. A qualification, even a D or E award at 0-grade, definitely improved the chances of finding a job. But during the 1970s a steady two in every five school leavers had no qualification at all. And after 1973 they had to wait another year, until they were 16, before they were allowed to leave. What was the point of being there, if they had nothing to show for it?

By the 1980s, in an effort to tackle some of these problems, changes were once again sweeping through Scotland's secondary schools. The belt was on the way out. New subjects and new ways of teaching were on the way in. And a new exam system was being prepared, to make sure that everyone would leave school with a qualification of some sort.

A Place to Live

In 1945 Scotland's housing problems looked as big as ever. Far too many Scottish soldiers were returning to slums. Hundreds of thousands of new houses would be needed. But a mad building scramble was not the answer. Between the wars there had been too much attention to quantity and not enough to quality. As a result, old slums had been replaced by new slums. For the future, Scotland would need quality as well as quantity to solve its housing problems.

Mammy's Got a Prefab

While Scotland's planners wrestled with the country's problems in 1945, the desperate need for new houses was met by prefabs, or prefabricated houses. These were made in sections in factories, then taken to the building site and fitted together. They were a clever way of building new homes very quickly. What's more, they gave peace-time work to factories that had been making aircraft or other war equipment. In next to no time, they were popping up all over Scotland like mushrooms in the night. Over four thousand appeared in Edinburgh, almost three thousand in Glasgow.

Prefabs such as those above, built at Mount Florida, Glasgow, were built as temporary houses, with a life-span of ten to twenty years. A few have survived into the present, for example at Hangingshaw in Glasgow's Mount Florida district, but most have vanished. Yet these 'stop-gap' houses are remembered fondly by the people who lived in them, for they had been designed with great care. That's why many playgrounds in 1945 rang to the excited boast
'Hay bab-a-ree-bab,
Ma mammy's got a prefab.'

The number one priority was the Clyde Valley, containing almost half of Scotland's population and with the tenement city of Glasgow at its heart. No other city in Europe was as jam-packed as Glasgow. Almost three-quarters of a million people were crammed into the city centre, equivalent to up to fifteen hundred people living in an area the same size as a football pitch!

The planners argued that the only answer was to move half a million people out of central Glasgow. But at the same time they argued that there should be a 'green belt' around Glasgow and other towns in the Clyde valley. No new building would be allowed on the green belt, which would stop the suburbs from sprawling all over the countryside.

But if a green belt was drawn around Glasgow, where could the people moving out of the centre be rehoused? The green belt still left enough space to house about half of them in new housing estates on the outskirts. The other half would have to be moved to completely new towns built well away from Glasgow.

The government liked this plan, and by 1947 it had created the green belt and given the go-ahead for the first new town. It would be about ten miles south of Glasgow, at a place called East Kilbride. The rebuilding of Scotland was under way.

Scotland's First New Town

East Kilbride was the first of five new towns built in Scotland since the war. The others are Glenrothes, Cumbernauld, Livingston and Irvine. Each one is unique, and they have all created strong feelings for or against. But it is agreed that building them was a bold and ambitious thing to do.

The idea behind the new towns was the 'garden city', which an Englishman called Ebenezer Howard had suggested around 1900. Howard saw the garden city as an answer to the problems of big industrial cities. It would be laid out on open countryside, with plenty of light, air and space. Home and work would be kept apart, so no-one would have to live next to a smoky, noisy factory. And the houses would be like cottages with their own garden, not blocks of flats or tenements.

The only place in Scotland that had been built on garden city lines was at Rosyth, for the naval dockyard workers. But Rosyth was small, with not much more than a thousand houses.

The planners designed East Kilbride so that there were six neighbourhoods grouped around a town centre. Each neighbourhood had its own local shops and schools, its own churches and play areas. Main roads ran round each neighbourhood, not through it. As a result, a shop was always within walking distance. And children could walk to their local primary school without having to cross any major roads.

Next, on land well away from the housing neighbourhoods, four industrial estates were created. And finally, in the middle of East Kilbride, a town centre began to emerge from the mud and dust of building sites. Here in a park a great billowing sheet of concrete arched over an olympic-length swimming pool. Here were the shopping arcades, cinemas and theatres, the sports centres, hotels and offices. Here was the heart of East Kilbride, designed to turn a group of neighbourhoods into a living, breathing town.

East Kilbride quickly proved that it could attract people and jobs. It grew so rapidly that the planners had to return to their drawing boards and make space for more houses. By 1985 it had become one of Scotland's largest towns, and was home for over 70,000 people.

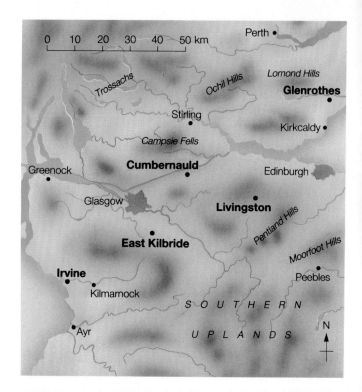

Top Map of Scotland's new towns *Middle* East Kilbride was a tiny village in the country until 1947. *Bottom* Modern East Kilbride is one of Scotland's largest towns.

A Tour of the New Towns

Glenrothes in Fife was chosen in 1948 as the site of Scotland's second new town. Built on open countryside, Glenrothes was to be a new-style mining town utterly different from the grimy mining villages of the past.

Glenrothes did not have an easy start in life. The mines around it needed fewer workers than expected. And the 'super-pit' at Rothes, the area's brightest hope, had to be abandoned. It was a bitter set-back for the new town.

But Glenrothes fought back, and began to build a new future for itself as a centre of Scotland's electronics industry. By the 1980s Glenrothes was half the size of East Kilbride. But its microchip factories and assembly lines had earned it a place in 'Silicon Glen', Scotland's own version of California's Silicon Valley.

Cumbernauld was the next town to be given the go-ahead in 1956. Fifteen miles north-east of Glasgow, it became one of the most talked about new towns of all time. 'There is nothing like it in Britain, or for that matter in the world' was the proud claim of the town's officials.

What made Cumbernauld so different? For a start, the town centre was built on top of a hill, and perched there like some strange modern fort. Houses huddled closely around the hill-top, almost all within walking distance of the town centre. It was a compact lay-out, but it was carefully designed. Most houses had some sunlight and a view of the hills rather than of their neighbour's house! And people and cars were kept safely apart, so that Cumbernauld had only a fifth of the accidents that any normal town suffered. Before long, architects and planners from all over the world were coming to see this newest of new towns. Most were impressed by what they saw.

No danger from traffic in this part of Cumbernauld

In 1962 Scotland's fourth new town was placed right outside the Clyde Valley at Livingston in West Lothian. The site was ideal for another garden city, for it was open country along the valley of the River Almond. And it was a good place for business, sitting astride the motorway and railway between Glasgow and Edinburgh. So an ambitious grid pattern of roads was planned around the town centre. As Livingston grew, it was easy to extent the grid and make room for more people.

Finally, in 1966, plans were announced for Irvine new town. It was on the Ayrshire coast, making it the first seaside new town in Britain. And unlike Scotland's other new towns, Irvine was not built on open countryside. There were villages, a harbour and the two old towns of Kilwinning and Irvine. For the new town to be a success, these separate communities would have to be welded.

Visitors to the new towns do not always like what they see. They complain that the buildings lack character, that the towns have no identity. But four in every five companies moving to Scotland choose to go to the new towns. And a quarter of a million Scots now live in the new towns. For them, life is a lot better than it was in the old towns and cities. They have been given a future, and are determined to make it work. The great new town experiment is finished, but it is also just beginning.

Irvine's marriage of old and new can be seen very clearly in the town centre shown in the photograph below. The old shopping streets are still there, but now they are linked to a brand new shopping centre that leaps across the River Irvine. The old town has had a heart transplant.

'A Desert wi' Windaes'

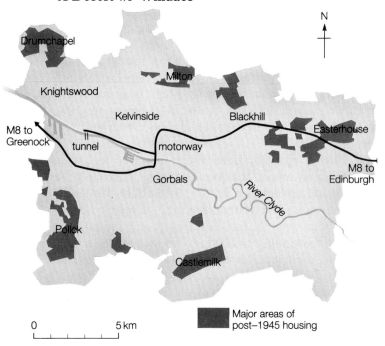

Above Map of Glasgow's post-war council housing schemes *Right* Frankie Vaughan talks to members of the 'Pak' gang, Easterhouse.

Around 1970 a famous singer called Frankie Vaughan took an interest in the problems of Glasgow's giant new housing schemes. He visited the housing schemes, followed by crowds of reporters and photographers, and tried to stop the gang warfare. He arranged truces, collected weapons and held meetings. But he saw that one of the biggest problems was the lack of facilities.

The new towns were built to help Glasgow by making it less crowded. But Glasgow's councillors still liked to think of it as 'the second city of the empire'. They did not want to see it shrink.

So while work began on the first new town at East Kilbride, Glasgow decided to build vast housing schemes on the outskirts of the city. There was not much space, because of the green belt and the hills around the city, so the houses would have to be packed in. But at least the city would be able to hold on to its citizens.

At the beginning of the 1950s work began on five huge schemes. The first were at Pollok and Priesthill to the west of the city. Next came Drumchapel to the north west, then Castlemilk to the south east, and finally Easterhouse to the east.

Each of these massive schemes was built to house between twenty-five and thirty thousand people. That made them bigger than towns like Stirling.

And they were five or six miles away from the centre of Glasgow. So they needed all the things a town needs, like shops, schools, cafes, pubs, churches, swimming pools and cinemas.

But it took years and years for these things to appear. So the schemes were nothing like towns. They were just houses, houses, houses, or what Billy Connolly called 'a desert wi' windaes.' They were miles from anywhere, and there was nothing to do. In less than ten years, they all had big problems of vandalism and were well-known for their gangs.

During the 1970s some action was at last taken. A township centre was built in Easterhouse in 1970. A community centre and swimming baths were built in Castlemilk after a twenty year wait. And after 1969 the council agreed to allow pubs to be built in the schemes. But many people no longer wanted to live in the schemes. By the 1980s, a quarter of the houses in Castlemilk and Drumchapel lay empty. It looked as though many might have to be demolished. There had to be better ways of solving Glasgow's housing problems.

Graffiti, Drumchapel, 1978

High Rise Dreams

By 1955 Glasgow had reached the green belt, and could not sprawl out any further. Yet hundreds of thousands of people still had to be rehoused. So the city at last accepted that it could no longer keep all its citizens. It started an 'overspill' policy, helping people to move out of Glasgow to new towns like Cumbernauld and to nearby towns like Johnstone and Barrhead. In this way, the city's·population was expected to fall from about one million to three-quarters of a million people.

Next, Glasgow looked inwards, and upwards. It could not spread out the way, but what was to stop it spreading up the way by building multi-storey tower blocks?

Glasgow's councillors, planners and architects had thought about high-rise houses in the past. In 1939 they visited New York. And in 1947 they visited Marseilles in the south of France to study one of the world's most famous multi-storey housing projects. It was the brainchild of a Swiss architect called Le Corbusier. Le Corbusier believed in a perfect future for the world, a 'Utopia'. And he thought he knew how to create it. The house, he said, was 'a machine for living in'. Like other machines, it should be standardized and mass-produced on a vast scale. He dreamt of 'vertical garden cities', massive blocks of flats soaring into the sky above an open countryside of grass and trees.

Le Corbusier's vision appealed to the visitors from Glasgow. They returned home and in 1948 ordered three ten-storey blocks of flats at Cardonald in the west of the city. They were finished in 1953 and called Moss Heights. These 'machines for living in' were not perfect: the lifts were so small that furniture had to be carried up ten storeys! But inside, the flats were roomy and comfortable, with central heating and fitted kitchens.

Below Le Corbusier's plan for central Paris in 1925. It was rejected.   *Bottom* Le Corbusier's vision reached Scotland in 1953: Moss Heights

The main reason why Glasgow had not ordered a lot of multi-storey blocks in the past had been expense. The higher the building, the higher the cost, and Glasgow was not a wealthy city. But by 1957 the government also saw high rise as a way of solving the nation's housing shortage without using up more land. So it agreed to give grants to councils that wanted to build multi-storey houses: the higher the building, the higher the grant. All over Scotland, towns and cities began to draw up plans for high-rise housing.

Tower Block Troubles

The old makes way for the new; Hutchesontown in the 1960s

The 1960s were years when Glasgow changed more quickly than at any time this century. First, the council would pick an area of slums that it wanted to clear, and call it a 'comprehensive development area'. Then the people who lived there were moved out, and the demolition squads arrived with their bulldozers and ball-and-chains. Amid clouds of dust, great crackling bonfires and roaring machinery, the old buildings were smashed and dragged to the ground. Once the site was cleared, lorries would begin to arrive with concrete slabs and beams. Cranes would swing slowly through the air, and a tower would begin to take shape. Sometimes it was just eight to ten storeys, sometimes fifteen or twenty. But often it would just keep rising, to twenty-five or thirty storeys, as though no-one knew how to stop the spinning cranes.

Finally, many of the tenants who had been moved out of slums could return to the new flats that had taken their place. People who had lived all their lives in an area of the city found that it had vanished without trace. The Gorbals was one of the first areas to go, then Pollokshaws, Govan and many others. In place of the tightly-packed tenements, two hundred tower blocks had been built by 1970.

For many people, life in the tower blocks has been a huge improvement on the tenements. They have comfortable, well-designed homes with the bonus of a wonderful view. But as the number of tower blocks increased, more and more problems appeared. It could be lonely in a high flat, and it seemed to be much harder to get to know neighbours. There were no corner shops for old people, just car parks and empty spaces.

Adam McNaughtan wrote the 'Jeely Piece Song' in 1967 about the differences between the tenements and tower blocks. Everyone knew exactly what he meant:

'Oh ye cannae fling pieces oot a twenty storey flat,
Seven hundred hungry weans'll testify to that.
If it's butter, cheese or jeely, if the breid is plain or pan,
The odds against it reaching earth are ninety-nine tae wan.

'Oh the first day ma saw flung oot a daud o' Hovis broon;
It came skytin' oot the windae and went up insteid o' doon.
Noo every twenty-seven hoors it comes back intae sight
'Cause ma piece went intae orbit and became a satellite.'

124

At Hutchesontown (right) the famous architect Sir Basil Spence designed two long 'slab blocks' twenty storeys high, perched on top of concrete stilts and with garden balconies.

It seemed to fit Le Corbusier's vision: a vertical garden city with the countryside rolling underneath it. But while the architect collected prizes, the people living there faced all sorts of problems. The wind whistled round the stilts and under the blocks, strongly enough to blow people off their feet. Inside, the long dark narrow corridors that ran along each floor were unpleasant and scary. The 'hanging gardens' of Hutchesontown didn't seem much like Utopia.

There were also some far more serious problems. Too many architects wanted to experiment with new building materials and methods that they did not understand. As a result some of the towers let in rain and wind. Bits fell off. Windows and doors jammed. People could not afford to switch on expensive heating systems and so flats became damp.

Lifts seemed to be constantly out of action, stranding people hundreds of feet off the ground. 'Each house is rather like a warm, comfortable, isolated cell' was the way one young mother described life in Glasgow's 31-storey Red Road flats in 1971. Vandalism and mugging became common, and reduced the life of the tenants to misery.

During the 1960s problems like these appeared all over the country. The government decided to stop giving grants for tower blocks, and the high-rise fashion came to an end. But by then, multi-storeys had been built all over Scotland. Many of them are well-built and handsome, and with proper care and attention they will have a long and useful life.

But the tower blocks have not solved all the problems they were meant to, and they have created new ones. Some of them are already unfit to live in and will have to be demolished.

Scotland has woken up from the high-rise dream.

Repairing the Damage

Demolition and 'comprehensive development' spread like a mania throughout Scotland during the 1950s and 1960s. Almost every town and city joined in. One of the first shopping centres, the Overgate centre in Dundee, appeared in 1958. It was soon followed by others in Cambuslang and elsewhere. Some towns, like Linlithgow, went further. In 1957 it began to modernize the whole town centre.

Many of the buildings demolished to make way for these schemes were rotting and worthless. But a lot of damage was done too. In 1959 many old buildings of great interest in Edinburgh's George Square were swept away. One of the oldest houses in Aberdeen's Union Street was knocked down in 1962 to make way for a supermarket. And too often the new buildings were ugly and badly designed.

More and more people began to think that the councils and the architects and the developers were behaving like vandals on a grand scale. But what could be done to stop them? One idea was to set up a Scottish Civic Trust, that could look after old buildings like a kind of watchdog. It began work in 1967.

Within a few weeks of starting in 1967, the Scottish Civic Trust was busy. The council in Stranraer wanted to pull down the sixteenth century Castle Kennedy in the centre of the town and put up a shopping centre. So the writer Maurice Lindsay and an architect went to have a look at the plan on behalf of the Civic Trust.

'Together, we crawled over the castle and quickly agreed that on no account should it be destroyed. An on-the-spot argument then developed with a local councillor, sent to support the views of his destructively-minded colleagues . . .

"Ma ancestors were tortured in yon castle .. an' that's why I want to see it dinged doon."

"On these grounds" said I, "you would claim that Edinburgh Castle ought also to be dinged doon and replaced with a car park."

"Ah'd be in favour o' that" said the elected representative.'

Fortunately, neither Castle Kennedy or Edinburgh Castle were 'dinged doon'.

Then in 1969 the government agreed to draw up a list of buildings all over Scotland that were too important to pull down. And by the 1980s several hundred local Civic Trusts had formed all over Scotland to watch for buildings in danger.

The buildings that had suffered most at the hands of the demolishers were the tenements. Condemned as slums, they had been torn down by the hectare. Many of them deserved no better. But lots were perfectly sound and dignified buildings. What's more, people liked them, especially when the alternative was to be stuck out in a scheme or up in the sky. So during the 1970s many tenements that had survived the storms of demolition were modernized and sandblasted clean.

As the planners, councils and architects had discovered, pulling them down was easy, but putting something better in their place was very hard.

New Ways And Old

In the years after 1945, the builders and planners changed the face of Scotland. But customs and habits changed too, as people began to live their lives in new ways.

The Church had always held an important place in Scottish life. In 1960 almost three quarters of Scots adults belonged to a church, compared with less than one quarter of English adults. But during the 1960s fewer and fewer people went to Protestant churches, and by the 1970s the Catholic churches too were facing decline. Some churches were converted into houses or even bars, others were demolished or left to crumble. And as religious belief and observance faded, the Scottish Sabbath became plain Sunday.

People sometimes blamed the fall in church attendances on television. Television was blamed again when attendances began to fall at Scotland's football grounds. Whatever the reason, people drifted away from the terraces all through the 1960s and 1970s, and found other ways to pass Saturday afternoons. Still, all Scotland could look back with pride to that day in 1967 when Glasgow Celtic became the first British club to win the European Cup. And by the 1980s there were signs that the crowds might be returning, to cleaner and safer grounds.

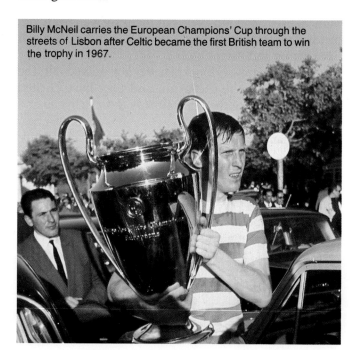

Billy McNeil carries the European Champions' Cup through the streets of Lisbon after Celtic became the first British team to win the trophy in 1967.

Street violence: a razor attack in Glasgow, 1960s

The General Assembly of the Church of Scotland

A 1980s wine bar in Leith

A new addition to Glasgow's skyline: a mosque by the river

Another Scottish custom returned for a while during the 1960s and 1970s – gang trouble. Fights might break out in football grounds, in dance halls, on buses, pubs, or in the streets. It was dangerous and frightening, but hard to stop. Some people thought that it was connected to drinking, like many other Scottish problems.

In 1978 the government decided to change the licensing laws that controlled Scottish pubs. The idea was to let them stay open longer than previously allowed, and to make drinking a bit more relaxed and civilised. It will be many years before the results of this bold experiment become clear. But the atmosphere in many pubs did change a great deal, and by the 1980s there were lots more wine bars, bistros, and continental-style cafes in Scottish towns and cities.

Finally, the new Scots. During the 1950s and 1960s, while hundreds of thousands of Scots were emigrating, other people were arriving to make Scotland their new home. Most came from England, others from Northern Ireland and the Irish Republic. But some came from further afield, and by 1981 there were around 50,000 Scots of Indian or Pakistani origin. It wasn't a large number compared to other parts of Britain, or compared with the 300,000 English in Scotland. But these new Scots soon made a big impact. Many started corner shops or restaurants, and soon a curry was as much of a Scottish tradition as haggis and chips. Others worked as doctors or chemists. In Glasgow the skyline was pierced by the silhouette of a mosque. Gradually, the new religions and languages, the new clothes and food, the new customs and ceremonies, mixed with the old. And who could doubt that, as a result, Scottish life was the richer?

Work to do . . .

1 Look at the graphs and charts on Scotland's health, and then put into words the main changes they show over the years since 1950. Why do you think these changes have happened?

2 Imagine going home from school through a thick 'smog'. Write a few paragraphs describing your journey.

3 Describe the ways in which schools have changed since 1945. Which changes do you think were best? Which do you think were worst? What changes would you most like to make in schools? Why?

4 Look closely at the photographs of tower blocks in Scotland. Then look at Le Corbusier's drawing of a tower block city. How similar or different would you say they are?

5 How many new towns were built in Scotland after 1945? Which are they? How many people now live in them? Which one: is built on a hill; includes two old towns; has roads on a grid pattern; turned from coal-mining to electronics; is the biggest and oldest new town?

On the Move

The Car Age

Top Improvements to the Loch Lomond road in the 1980s. The old road can be seen to the left of the new one. *Above* Motorways meet at the Baillieston Interchange

For years after they first appeared in Scotland, motor cars were just a rich man's toy. Even by 1939 cars were still a luxury for most Scots, and only one person in thirty owned one. But after the war the number of cars on the roads soared, until by 1985 there were over one and a quarter million, or one for every four people. Scotland had entered the car age.

To make way for cars, the face of Scotland had to be changed. Roads and bridges built for slow-moving horses and coaches were widened and straightened out, with thousands of new bridges across rivers and streams. Some famous bends vanished, like the Devil's Elbow in Glenshee. Sometimes the route followed by an old road was too bendy, bumpy and hilly to be of use at all for motor cars. If so, it was abandoned to walkers and the weeds, like the old road across Rannoch Moor, and a brand new road was pushed through.

Long detours round estuaries or sea-lochs, or long waits for ferries, were removed by building new bridges. The Forth was spanned by a suspension bridge in 1964, making a stark modern contrast to the massive leaping fretwork of the nearby railway bridge. The Tay was bridged at Dundee in 1966, then the Clyde at Erskine. Further north, new bridges were thrown across the Cromarty and Beauly Firths, and across the mouth of Loch Leven at Ballachulish.

To cope with the constant stream of traffic between Scotland's main towns and cities, work began on a network of motorways. 'Motorway' was not a word that many people had heard of during the 1950s, but by 1964 Scotland's first stretch of four-lane highway had been opened in Fife.

By 1985 over two hundred miles of motorway were in use, and Scotland even had its own 'spaghetti junction' a few miles south of Glasgow, where motorways are piled on stilts one above the other.

Despite their noise and smell, the motorways have brought many advantages. They are faster than any other sort of road, and also safer. They have eased the suffering of towns like Stirling, whose centres once were choked with traffic impatient to pass through. And many plants and animals have found a safe home along the verges, embankments and cuttings. Perhaps, some time in the future, people will want to protect the motorway verges just as nowadays they want to protect the hedgerows!

Cities in a Jam

Cars made their biggest impact in the towns and cities. Like the tide, they flooded from the suburbs into the centre in the morning, and back out in the evening. Roads were jammed by parked cars, making things even more difficult for through traffic. Aberdeen tried to keep traffic out of the centre by making Anderson Drive into a ring road. Dundee built a new ring road, the Kingsway, around the north of the city. Edinburgh tried to control parking, and in 1962 became the first Scottish city to put up parking meters.

Glasgow, still in the grip of its redevelopment fever, decided in 1965 to go for a system of urban motorways – fast-flowing traffic arteries running around the heart of the city.

By the 1980s much of Glasgow's new road system was in use. An expressway ran along the north side of the Clyde then dived into a tunnel under the river at Whiteinch. And the motorway from Edinburgh swept through Easterhouse and past Blackhill into the north of the city centre, curled south and plunged into a deep concrete cutting at Charing Cross, passed within a few hundred yards of the city centre, then strode high over the Clyde on the Kingston Bridge, and finally banked steeply and headed off due west for Paisley, Greenock and the Erskine Bridge.

Above A bird's eye view of Glasgow looking towards the Kingston Bridge.
Right The last tram parade through Glasgow's wet streets in 1962

Edinburgh, too, began to draw up plans for urban motorways. One idea was to turn Princes Street into a three-level expressway. Another was to run a motorway along Princes Street Gardens and round the New Town. But roads like these were very expensive and caused a great deal of damage. In Glasgow seven thousand houses had to be knocked down because they were in the way. Edinburgh's plans would have caused even more damage, and there was such an uproar of protest that in 1969 the plans were dropped.

Another effect of cars was to squeeze trams out of existence. During the 1950s they vanished from the streets of Dundee, Edinburgh and Aberdeen. The last stronghold, Glasgow, fell in 1962, when a farewell procession of tramcars made its way through streets crowded with onlookers and trundled into memory.

Scotland's trams were scrapped in the name of modernity. The tramlines were torn from the street and the space was handed over to cars and buses. The odd thing was that all over Europe dozens of cities had reached the opposite conclusion. They thought that trams were much better than cars or buses at moving people around crowded cities, quickly, quietly, and cleanly. From Warsaw to Berlin, Cologne to Geneva, trams were being improved and modernized.

At least Glasgow had other types of public transport to fall back on. The railway lines looping through its northern and southern suburbs were electrified in the early 1960s. And in 1980 the city's underground railway was back in use after being completely modernized. But in Scotland's other towns and cities, the victory of motor cars and buses was complete.

Modern farming in Scotland: a few machines can do the work of many hands

In Scotland's countryside there were no traffic jams or rush-hours, but motor cars did change people's lives. From the 1930s onwards it had been common for farmers to own cars. But the farm labourers who worked for them could not afford a car, and felt more and more stranded.

Fewer people wanted to work in the countryside. And combine harvesters, tractors and other motorized machines meant that fewer were needed. In 1950 there were about one hundred and twenty thousand people working on Scotland's farms, but by 1980 two-thirds of them had left and only forty thousand remained. Village shops and schools had to close, making town life seem even more attractive. The countryside had never been so empty.

After the war, many farm labourers started 'voting with their feet' by leaving the countryside and moving to the towns. Farmers had difficulty in finding people to work for them. Here is a Borders farmer in 1950 describing how he had to travel to a town eighty miles away to interview a man he wanted to employ as a ploughman:

'It was all right while I spoke to him, and he seemed quite willing to take the job. Then his two daughters came in – he was a widower – and asked how far the cottage was from the nearest town, and what the bus services were like and so on and when I told them (the nearest town was 15 miles away) they flatly refused to come. So of course he couldn't come either'.

Railways Axed

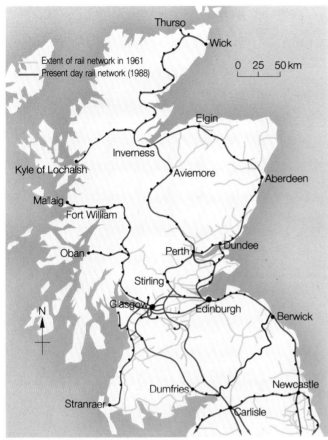

A map of Scotland's shrinking railway network.

West coast electric: a London-Glasgow express

Abandoned railway line at Grandtully

The spread of motor cars, and a big fall in the number of people working on farms, made life very hard for railway lines serving country areas. Dozens of branch lines were losing money hand over fist. The railways decided to ask a businessman called Dr Beeching to look at the problem, and in 1963 he gave his answer: branch lines would have to be closed.

Soon the thud of the axe was being heard all over Scotland. Fraserburgh, Crieff, Forfar were chopped from the railway network. In 1965 the line from Dumfries to Stranraer was closed. In 1969 the 'Waverley Route', running from Carlisle through Hawick and Galashiels was axed. Hundreds of stations were closed, from the smallest of country halts to the splendid terminus at Glasgow St Enoch.

The Beeching axe caused a lot of anger, and the government did not accept all of his plan. He wanted to close all the railway lines north of Inverness, to Thurso, Wick and across to Kyle of Lochalsh. But the government was persuaded that these lines were vital to local people, especially in winter, and agreed to pay for their losses. Still, Scotland's railways were almost halved between 1957 and 1985, from over 3200 miles to just 1700 miles.

But the Beeching plan was not just about closing, cutting and scrapping. It let the railways concentrate on improving the main lines. By 1974 the line from Glasgow to London had been electrified, cutting the journey time to five hours. And by 1978 high speed trains had brought Edinburgh within five hours of London. So by the 1980s people could no longer take a train up a branch line into the countryside. But train journeys between the big cities were faster than ever.

131

Aberdeen Airport: *Above* in the 1980s *Opposite* In the 1940s

Scotland had taken to the air during the 1930s, with regular passenger flights around the Highlands and Islands and to cities like Belfast, Birmingham and London. But the war gave flying a tremendous boost. New planes were developed, jet engines and radar were invented, and thousands of pilots were trained. At Prestwick in Ayrshire, Renfrew near Glasgow, Turnhouse near Edinburgh and Dyce near Aberdeen, old bumpy grass landing strips were buried under strong concrete runways. With these four major airports and many smaller ones, Scotland was well-set to start new peace-time passenger services.

At first the plans were modest. Terminal buildings were just a few low wooden huts, and a handful of aircraft arrived and left each day. But from small beginnings, air travel grew so fast that the airports could hardly keep up.

Aberdeen's airport started small but grew steadily, until oil was discovered. Then, Dyce turned into the

fastest-growing airport in Britain. For every passenger using it in 1972, there were ten in 1982. One and a half million passengers each year crowded through the new terminal. Many of them, as in most airports, were businessmen in dark suits carrying suitcases. But there were also lots of leather-jacketed men carrying kit-bags. They were oil-rig crews, being ferried back and forth on helicopters, which constantly throbbed and clattered through the sky above the Granite City.

In Scotland's central belt it might have made sense to build one central airport serving Glasgow and Edinburgh. But both cities wanted their own, and no-one was willing to close Prestwick down the Ayrshire coast. So Prestwick was set aside for transatlantic flights, and Glasgow and Edinburgh pushed ahead with their own plans.

At Turnhouse, a new terminal building was built in 1956 to cope with 75,000 passengers each year. But less than ten years later half a million people each year

Scotland's largest airport was opened at Dyce on Saturday. Here we have a general view of the airport, with a plane of the Royal Air Force flight in the foreground.

were passing through! By the 1970s Turnhouse was so crowded that another new terminal building was needed, and a new runway.

For a while, Prestwick too was busy. It was hardly ever fogbound, and its long runway could cope with the biggest jets. A regular stream of Scots flew out of Prestwick to visit relatives in Canada and America, and almost as many Canadians and Americans arrived at Prestwick to visit 'the old country'. But Prestwick was too far away from the big cities to be popular. And its fog-free record became less important once aircraft could be guided safely to the ground through all but the thickest of fogs by electronic instruments. By the 1980s it was still Scotland's transatlantic airport, but its terminal building and car parks were strangely quiet.

Renfrew was the busiest airport of all. But by the 1960s there was just not enough room for more terminals, and the runway had become too short for bigger aircraft. One plane that had landed in an emergency did not have enough space to take off again, and had to be dismantled and moved to a longer runway! So in 1966 Glasgow's airport was moved from Renfrew to Abbotsinch, just north of Paisley. Here there was room to expand, and by 1980 Glasgow had the fourth busiest airport in Britain after Heathrow, Gatwick and Manchester.

So by the 1980s flying had become a part of everyday life in Scotland. Jets shuttled back and forward to London every hour, and regular travellers just hopped aboard as if they were catching a bus. Lots of people flew to the sun every year for summer holidays in Spain, Greece, Portugal or even further afield. Seven million passengers passed through Scotland's airports each year, and the numbers were increasing all the time. Hardly anyone bothered to look up as the great silver birds thundered overhead. It was hard to believe that only fifty years had passed since the flying circus could bring thousands of people running to a grass field for the thrill of a five shilling joy-ride.

Work to do . . .

1 Motorways are designed so that all traffic enters and leaves them from the left. Imagine two motorways crossing each other, one above the other. As you drive towards the intersection, you have to be able to continue the way you are going, or to change direction and go left, right, or back the way you came. Now try to design the intersection (hint: junctions like this are sometimes called clover leaf junctions).

2 Try to find out – from maps, older people, or your own local knowledge – if any abandoned railways exist in your area. If so, try to discover when it was built, what it was called, and when it was closed. Perhaps your class could make a photographic record of what remains, such as bridges, stations, signs, cuttings and embankments.

3 Copy the aerial photograph of Aberdeen Airport on a piece of paper. Then see if you can label these things on your drawing: runway; apron; hangar; terminal building; car park.

Highland Hopes

Sloy hydro-electric station on the banks of Loch Lomond

Tom Johnston's Plan

Emigration, neglect and decay stretched far back in Highland history, and the war made little difference. Some new roads and piers were built, and many new telephone lines were laid, so that soldiers could be transported more easily to training areas. But by the end of the war moving around was still very difficult, especially by sea.

'Take Little Loch Broom and Loch Broom, for example' said one observer describing Highland travel problems around 1947: 'these north-western lochs had a daily steamer in the year 1900; now it is once in three weeks; then it was possible to cross the Minch from these lochs to Stornoway and back again; now, to get from Little Loch Broom to Stornoway, one must catch the mail car at 8.30 am, drive to Braemore, change to a bus and drive to Garve, catch the 1 o'clock train from Garve to Kyle of Lochalsh, board the steamer, and reach Stornoway at 8.15 pm. One finishes up 45 miles away from where one started twelve hours before.'

Nor did the war stop people from leaving. Many young women from the Highlands and Islands went to work in lowland and English factories, and decided not to return. And fishermen still left the islands for work in the Royal Navy and Merchant Navy. Islay produced so many sailors that people called it the 'nursery of sea captains'. Many of them, too, did not return.

One man determined to break this long unhappiness in the north was the Labour MP Tom Johnston. He believed that the government could bring the Highlands to life by building hydro-electric power stations. The Americans had shown the way during the 1930s, using hydro-electric schemes to revive their depressed south. If it worked in the Tennessee Valley, then he thought it could also work in the Highlands of Scotland.

Johnston's chance to do something came during the war. In 1941 Prime Minister Churchill made him Secretary of State for Scotland, the most powerful politician in the country. He acted quickly, and by 1943 had pushed the government into creating the North of Scotland Hydro-Electric Board. Now his hopes of Highland revival, of progress through electricity, could be put to the test.

Power from the Glens

As soon as the war ended, the Hydro-Board got to work. Its first scheme was at Loch Sloy in the mountains west of Loch Lomond. A huge concrete dam, 55 metres high and 365 metres long, was built to collect water. Then the water was led 3 kilometres along a tunnel bored through the rocky heart of Ben Vorlich. It emerged high on the slopes above Loch Lomond, and then thundered down four great steel pipelines to the power station at Inveruglas Bay. There, the water set the turbines spinning, producing electricity that was taken away on tall pylons marching over the hills. Power from the glens!

Sloy was just the beginning. Next, the Hydro-Board moved north to the Tummel Valley, then even further north to Glen Affric. Within twenty years, it had built eighty-four dams and fifty-six power stations. Glen after glen was flooded, rivers stopped flowing, and dams, power stations, pipes and pylons spread across the Highlands.

The Hydro-Board's job was not just to make electricity. It also had to make sure that anyone who wanted to use electricity was connected. That was a tall order. The land was rough, the people remote. In 1945 only one Highland farm in six, and one croft in a hundred, had an electricity supply. To solve this problem, the Board sold electricity to the south, then ploughed the profits into a network for the north. It was a clever way of diverting money to the Highlands, and if the southerners were not too pleased, the Highlanders were delighted! Thousand of miles of cable were strung on pylons and posts to towns and villages all over the north. Submarine cables carried power to the islands. By the 1960s, electricity had reached over ninety-eight per cent of the people who wanted it.

Through its efforts, the Hydro-Board won a warm place in the hearts of Highlanders. And although its pipes and pylons were an eyesore, it tried hard to limit the damage it caused. Many of the power stations were hidden from sight in underground chambers, or were handsome stone buildings. Fish were helped past the dams in lifts and watery step-ladders. And thousands of tourists came to admire the great feats of civil engineering.

But despite its achievements, the Hydro-Board did not stop Highland decline. People drifted away all through the 1950s. New jobs did not appear. And by the 1960s the Hydro-Board had used all the best sites for generating electricity. In future it would have to import from the south most of the power it supplied. Tom Johnston's hopes for a great Highland revival had not yet happened. It was time to try something else.

A Highland Experiment

In 1965 Highland hopes were raised again, when the Highlands and Islands Development Board was set up. This Board was the creation of William Ross, the new Labour government's Secretary of State of Scotland. The Highlanders, Ross told the House of Commons, were on Scotland's conscience. The Highland Board would help to right the wrongs of the past. The government would give it money to help industry, fishing and agriculture. Its job was to improve conditions in the Highlands, and stop the constant emigration.

The new Board decided that the most urgent task was to attract new industry. It wanted to create 'growth-centres' in Caithness, around Fort William, and on the Moray Firth. It dreamt of vast developments near Inverness, and the population soaring from thirty thousand to a quarter of a million in ten years. In 1966 it was delighted when the government decided to build a new nuclear reactor at Dounreay on the northern Caithness coast. And there were more celebrations in 1968 when an aluminium company agreed to build a smelter at Invergordon, creating a thousand new jobs.

The best news of all came in 1971, when new figures showed that the population of the Highlands and Islands had stopped falling, and was increasing for the first time in a hundred years. The Highland experiment appeared to be working.

During the 1970s, the oil business came to the north, and the population of the Highlands rose even further. The Board started to take more interest in small local businesses. It helped to set up a few community co-operatives in the Western Isles and Orkney. Potters, jewellers and other craft-workers were given some help, and in 1981 a new craft centre called Highland Craftpoint was opened at Beauly.

No. 43,200 ∗ ∗ ∗ WEDNESDAY, DECEMBER 30, 1981

Invergordon closure stuns Highlands

By ALEX WATTIE, Our Industrial Correspondent

Front entrance to Invergordon smelter . . . soon the gates close for good.

The prospects of substantial industrial development in the Highlands were killed yesterday, perhaps until the end of the century, with the announcement that the Invergordon aluminium smelter is to close tomorrow with the loss of 890 jobs.

The suddenness of the announcement, surely the swiftest plant closure Scotland has experienced since the war, and the brutal implications of a shut-down on Hogmanay, left the country stunned.

At the end of a year of industrial tragedy for Scotland Mr George Younger, the

Secretary of State, who made the closure announcement in Glasgow, encapsulated the disaster when he said:

"I would rate this as being almost as serious for Invergordon, perhaps more so, as Linwood was for Renfrewshire. It is that sort of scale. Nine hundred jobs for Invergordon is a profound disaster."

The simple arithmetic of the closure goes beyond 890 jobs. Probably 700 more jobs in the

Top Dounreay nuclear site near Thurso in Caithness *Above* December 30, Eve 1981: more bad news at 'the end of a year of industrial tragedy'

But some people felt that the Board was still too interested in attracting 'big fish' to its growth-centres. They complained that these growth-centres were many miles away from the crofting areas in the north-west, and would not stop people from leaving them. And they wondered why these big industries should be the top priority for the Highlands, when they were declining in the rest of the country.

In 1979 the worst fears began to come true when the big pulp-mill at Corpach near Fort William closed, throwing almost five hundred people out of work. And in 1981 the aluminium smelter at Invergordon, which had been open for only ten years, announced that it too was losing money and would have to close. With those two great hammer-blows, the whole Highland economy was sent reeling. And the Highland Board's idea of growth-centres was knocked flat.

The older industries at least gave some comfort. Tweed had gone out of style during the 1970s, but by the 1980s it was back in fashion. The mills and workshops of Harris and Lewis could hardly keep up with the demand. And finally, there was the land and the sea.

Contrasts in forestry *Left* Mixed trees in Glen Affric *Right* Land prepared for long straight lines of trees on the island of Mull

On the land, the biggest changes were made by the Forestry Commission. Its plantations spread quickly after the war, from the Borders to Sutherland, and by 1980 it had trebled the area covered by trees. So much of its work was in Scotland that in 1978 it moved headquarters from London to Edinburgh.

The Forestry Commission's favourite tree was the Sitka Spruce, which grows straight and fast. But a forest of sitkas, row upon row for miles in every direction, is very unnatural. It is dark and quiet, and holds no attraction for wildlife.

So gradually the Forestry Commission began to use a variety of trees in its forests. It stopped planting everything in rows and squares. The natural Scottish woodland, of pine, birch, oak, rowan and elder, was given a chance to survive. Around Loch Lubnaig, in Glen Croe, in Glen Affric and elsewhere, the Forestry Commission showed that it could improve the landscape rather than ruin it.

By the 1980s well over a tenth of Scotland was being used to grow trees. That was far more than in England. But it was far less than in most European countries. The problem was that the land was being used for other things. More than a tenth of Scotland was taken up with grouse moors. People paid a lot of money to lean against a shooting butt and shoot grouse out of the sky. Then there were a quarter of a million red deer roaming the great estates. People paid a lot to shoot them too. The Highland Board wanted to see some of this land turned over to forestry. But when it tried, it found it had no power.

The Board had more success in encouraging fishing. The east coast inshore boats from Aberdeen and Peterhead were busy enough. But the Western Isles and Shetland needed help. So during the 1960s the Board built up the fleets at Stornoway and Shetland. Twenty-five new trawlers were ordered, bringing work to little boatbuilders from Argyll to Shetland. Skippers, engineers and crews were trained. Within a few years, a thousand jobs had been made or saved, and fishing was looking a lot healthier in the north and west of Scotland.

But the biggest and most hopeful change in Scottish fishing has been the increase in quality and luxury products. Prawns and lobsters brought prosperity to Scalpay and Eriskay. Mallaig handles countless tonnes of prawns (scampi). Crabs, shrimp, and scallops are landed all round the coast. Trout farms have sprung up, and for a few weeks each summer the salmon are netted as they return from the ocean to their Scottish river. The days are long past when Scottish herring were packed off in barrels to Germany and Russia. Now, Scottish lobsters are flown to Paris and London, and Scottish prawns are flown to Spain and New York.

Mallaig, 1987. This catch includes prawns, halibut, skate, and haddock.

Above Gaelic protest sign on the road to the Isles, 'Up with the Gaelic language!' *Above right* Rubbish dumped near West Highland tourist spot

Below 1960s brochure for Aviemore, summer and winter centre

Finally, there was tourism. Sir Walter Scott had set the fashion in the nineteenth century. But after 1945 the trickle of Highland tourists turned into a steady stream. In the early 1960s the first tourist centre in the Highlands was built at Aviemore. Ski-slopes appeared on Cairngorm, Glenshee, Glencoe and the Lecht. The Highland Board backed new hotels on Mull and Barra. By the 1980s a quarter of a million passengers and a hundred thousand cars a year were crossing the sea to Skye.

Tourism has become one of the most important Highland industries, and brings prosperity to the remotest corners. But it also brings problems. In 1970 a clean-up in the Cairngorms filled three hundred and seventy sackfuls of litter in a single weekend. Paths and tracks spread across the hills. The Highlands are one of the last great wildernesses in Europe. It would be a tragedy if people destroyed what they came to enjoy.

Work to do . . .

1 Who was Tom Johnston? How did he hope to bring life to the Highlands? How successful do you think he was?
2 Describe in your own words what the HIDB is and what it has tried to do. If you were in charge of it, how would you try to improve things in the Highlands?
3 Look at the two photographs of forestry schemes. Imagine a visit to each of them, and then prepare a short report that describes their sights, sounds, and smells.

A Nation of Culture

The Edinburgh Festival. Fireworks burst over Princes Street Gardens.

In the summer of 1947, for the first time since the war, the nations of Europe came together in a great festival of the arts. This International Festival of Music and Drama was a celebration of peace, and of the defeat of barbarism by civilization. And Scotland had an extra reason for celebrating, because the festival was held in Edinburgh.

Edinburgh's Lord Provost, Sir John Falconer, was enthusiastic about the idea of a festival and issued a warm welcome. 'Edinburgh', he said, 'will surrender herself to the visitors and hopes that they will find in all the performances a sense of peace and inspiration with which to refresh their souls . . . We wish to provide the world with a centre where year after year, all that is best in music, drama and the visual arts can be seen and heard . . .'

Europe had been starved of first-class music and drama. The old festival cities, like Salzburg and Bayreuth, were still recovering from the war. And Edinburgh had a line-up of great talent. Kathleen Ferrier sang with the Vienna Philharmonic Orchestra. Arthur Schnabel played the piano and Pierre Fournier the cello. Margot Fonteyn danced with the Sadler's Wells Ballet. So visitors flocked to the city, and the first festival was a tremendous success.

After 1947, a three-week long Edinburgh festival was held every year. There was music and drama, opera and dance. There was a Film Festival, too, with films from almost every country in the world. The art galleries held big exhibitions. A Military Tattoo took shape in 1950, with marching troops, skirling bagpipes, and spotlights sweeping the castle esplanade. A Television Festival became another big attraction.

Then there was the Fringe, an unofficial festival of performers who wanted to join the fun. By the 1980s, well over three hundred theatre groups and companies came from around the world to take part in the Fringe. Theatres and halls became so scarce that bus-stations, canteens, warehouses, and even caravans were pressed into use for performances.

Many other towns and cities in Europe now have their own festivals. Some spend far more than Edinburgh on building top-class facilities and on attracting the best performers. But the Edinburgh Festival is still unique. 'Year after year, all that is best' remains its aim, and it is hard to aim higher than that.

Big Screen, Small Screen

The Edinburgh Festival was like a window on the world, giving Scotland a glimpse of art and drama from many other countries. But it only lasted for three weeks, and no matter how popular it was only a small part of all Scotland had a chance to come and look.

That changed in 1952, when the BBC began to broadcast television programmes in Scotland. Only about forty thousand people in all Scotland had a 'telly' in 1952. But in 1953 there was a crowd around almost every television in the country to watch the coronation of a new Queen, Elizabeth the Second. That made most people want their own TV, and by 1960 there were a million. Before long almost every house in Scotland had a 'box in the corner', an electronic window on the world in their own living room.

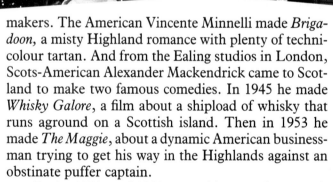

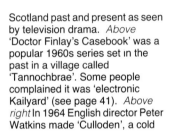

Scotland past and present as seen by television drama. *Above* 'Doctor Finlay's Casebook' was a popular 1960s series set in the past in a village called 'Tannochbrae'. Some people complained it was 'electronic Kailyard' (see page 41). *Above right* In 1964 English director Peter Watkins made 'Culloden', a cold look at Scottish history. *Right* Vivien Heilbron played Chris in 'Sunset Song', a series made in 1971. It was based on a classic novel by Lewis Grassic Gibbon. *Far right* Robbie Coltrane in 'Tutti Frutti', a 1987 series about a faded rock and roll band touring Scotland, written by John Byrne.

At first there was no choice but to watch BBC. But in 1957 a Canadian called Roy Thomson was given the go-ahead to start a commercial channel called Scottish Television or STV. Thomson already owned dozens of newspapers including the *Scotsman* in Edinburgh. And in Canada he owned a string of radio and television stations. He was certain STV would make a profit, and offered shares to hundreds of people in Scotland. Almost everyone turned down the chance. But when STV began, the profits poured in even faster than Roy Thomson had expected. Advertisers queued up to buy time on the channel. 'You know' said Thomson to his neighbours in Edinburgh, 'it's just like having a licence to print your own money!' He made a million pounds in the first year, and within a few years had made enough to buy the *Sunday Times* and become a Fleet Street press baron: Lord Thomson of Fleet. It showed just how powerful television had become in only a few years.

As television spread, cinemas started to close all over Scotland. Some were demolished to make way for shops, others were luckier and found new life as bingo halls. But young people still went to the cinema, and most of the films they watched came from America.

Scotland seldom appeared on the cinema's silver screen except in the work of American or English film-makers. The American Vincente Minnelli made *Brigadoon,* a misty Highland romance with plenty of technicolour tartan. And from the Ealing studios in London, Scots-American Alexander Mackendrick came to Scotland to make two famous comedies. In 1945 he made *Whisky Galore*, a film about a shipload of whisky that runs aground on a Scottish island. Then in 1953 he made *The Maggie,* about a dynamic American businessman trying to get his way in the Highlands against an obstinate puffer captain.

In the 1970s and 1980s something new happened. Scottish film-makers began to appear and to attract people to the cinema. Bill Douglas made three films using memories of his own life: *My Childhood, My Ain Folk,* and *My Way Home.* Bill Bryden's film *Ill Fares the Land,* was about the people of St Kilda abandoning their island.

Most popular of the new film-makers was Bill Forsyth. *Gregory's Girl* was a warm and funny film about growing up in a Scottish new town. And *Local Hero* was about an American oil company trying to buy a village and bay in the Highlands as a site for an oil terminal. 'Dreamland', says the mad scientist played by Rikki Fulton, as he plays with his models of plans to destroy the village. Nobody was quite sure why, but Scottish film-making had suddenly come to life.

139

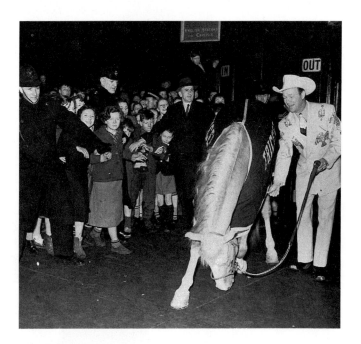

Scotland and cinema. *Left* Stars visiting Scotland in the 1950s could always be sure of a big welcome. Here, Roy Rogers and Trigger are greeted at Waverley Station, Edinburgh in 1954. *Above* 'Local Hero', 1983, and a Highland village awaits oil money

The Written Word

In 'The Poet's Pub' Below, painted in 1980, the artist Sandy Moffat imagines some of Scotland's leading poets gathered together in an Edinburgh pub – perhaps the Mitre or the Abbotsford. At the centre of the group, with pipe in hand, sits Hugh MacDiarmid. To his left Sydney Goodsir Smith (a New Zealander who spent much of his life in Edinburgh) raises his hand in the air, while the Orcadian George Mackay Brown crouches over his glass of beer. On the left sit Norman MacCaig and Edwin Morgan, and to the right stands Robert Garioch. The Lewisman Iain Crichton Smith sits at the back of the group, and to the rear stands Sorley MacLean or Somhairle MacGill-Eain from Raasay, a towering figure in twentieth-century Scottish Gaelic poetry and culture.

The author Muriel Spark Right was born and educated in Edinburgh. She has lived for most of her life in London and Italy, but one of her most famous novels – 'The Prime of Miss Jean Brodie' – is set in a girls' school in Edinburgh.

The Eden Court Theatre in Inverness Below right has encouraged theatre companies and musicians to travel north on tour. Over the last twenty-five years Scotland has depended on just a few theatre companies to set high standards. The Glasgow Citizens' Theatre and the Traverse Theatre in Edinburgh have led the way, and have also done much to support new Scottish playwrights.

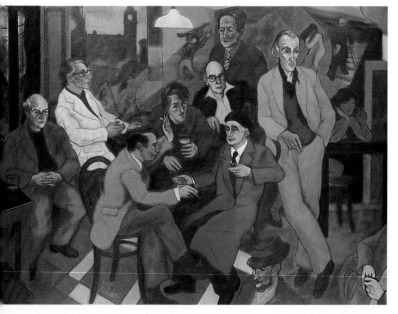

A Scottish Opera

During the 1950s energy from the Edinburgh Festival began to pulse round Scottish music. The Scottish National Orchestra became full-time and raised its standards. Orchestras and choirs sprang to life in many schools. The BBC in Scotland took far more interest in music and improved its own Scottish Symphony Orchestra. And in 1962 the first small steps were taken to create Scottish Opera.

Opera is a difficult and expensive thing to perform well. But Alexander Gibson, a musician from Motherwell, was steeped in it. He had trained in Scotland and London, and worked with the Sadler's Wells Opera. In 1960 he had become the first Scottish-born director of the Scottish National Orchestra. His idea in 1962 was to bring some opera singers to Glasgow, and put on a few performances in the King's Theatre.

He began with Puccini's popular opera *Madame Butterfly*. Audiences liked it, and so did the newspaper critics. So the next year Gibson drew up a slightly bigger programme for Glasgow and Edinburgh. The year after, it grew again and took in Aberdeen. And in 1967 Scottish opera was invited to the Edinburgh Festival, where the world could see the progress it had made.

A great act of faith came in 1975, when Scottish Opera decided to make a permanent home. It chose the Theatre Royal in Glasgow, a little gem of a theatre, and raised many millions of pounds to restore the building's splendour. And from its new home it took opera on tour. It travelled the country from Ayr to Elgin, from Kelso to Lochgelly. It was invited abroad, as a true International Company. All Scotland could take pride.

Fine Arts in Scotland

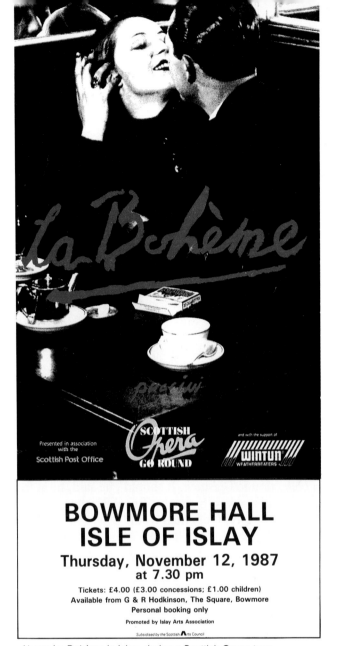

Above *La Bohème* in Islay, during a Scottish Opera tour

Works by two of Scotland's best known artists: *Right* 'Entrance for a Red Temple, No. I' by Alan Davie

Below A model by Eduardo Paolozzi for a sculpture called 'Hamlet in the Japanese Style'.

Winter Sea IV, painted by Joan Eardley at the north-east fishing village of Catterline. Eardley came from Sussex, but settled in Glasgow where she painted many scenes of slum life in the 1950s. Many of her later paintings show Catterline in stormy weather.

A Home for the Burrell Collection

All Scotland could take pride, too, when the splendours of the Burrell Collection at last went on show in 1984. It had taken forty years to find a home, for Sir William Burrell had laid down strict conditions when he gave his art collection to Glasgow. It should , he said, be at least sixteen miles away from the Royal Exchange in the centre of the city. Only then would it be a safe distance from the smoky dirt of Glasgow's air.

But Glasgow had cleaned itself up a lot, and after Burrell died in 1958 the search for a good home moved closer to the city. Finally in 1967 the Pollock Estate and House were gifted to the city. And in 1971 the architect Barry Gasson won a competition to design the building for the collection.

Below A home for the Burrell Collection

Gasson created another work of art. His building sat in a corner of parkland with glass walls separating trees on one side from tapestries and stained glass on the other. Gothic arches and windows were built into fresh pink sandstone walls. Complete rooms from Burrell's old home at Hutton Castle were rebuilt around a spacious courtyard.

When the Burrell Collection opened in 1983, the response was overwhelming. Within a year it had replaced Edinburgh Castle as Scotland's main tourist attraction. It was a great art collection, but to Scotland it was more than that. Scotland's industries had measured themselves against the world. So had her science. They had left a great legacy of wealth, in buildings, in art and in the ambitions of the country. And with that legacy, the world might still come to take the measure of Scotland.

Work to do . . .

1 When did the Edinburgh Festival begin? Make a list of all the different types of things you could see at the Festival nowadays. What would you most like to see?
2 Who described what as a 'licence to print your own money'?
3 Imagine you have been offered a chance to make a film in Scotland. The film must be based on some event in Scotland's history over the last 100 years, but the characters can be real or invented. What event would you pick, and how would you make it into a film? Work out the size of cast you would need, and the number of locations you would have to visit.

Index